T0311686

Cambridge Elements

Elements in Cognitive Linguistics
edited by
Sarah Duffy
Northumbria University
Nick Riches
Newcastle University

THE MANY FACES OF CREATIVITY

Exploring Synaesthesia through a Metaphorical Lens

Sarah Turner
Coventry University
Jeannette Littlemore
University of Birmingham

Shaftesbury Road, Cambridge CB2 8EA, United Kingdom

One Liberty Plaza, 20th Floor, New York, NY 10006, USA

477 Williamstown Road, Port Melbourne, VIC 3207, Australia

314–321, 3rd Floor, Plot 3, Splendor Forum, Jasola District Centre,
New Delhi – 110025, India

103 Penang Road, #05–06/07, Visioncrest Commercial, Singapore 238467

Cambridge University Press is part of Cambridge University Press & Assessment,
a department of the University of Cambridge.

We share the University's mission to contribute to society through the pursuit of
education, learning and research at the highest international levels of excellence.

www.cambridge.org
Information on this title: www.cambridge.org/9781108971362

DOI: 10.1017/9781108974813

First published 2023

A catalogue record for this publication is available from the British Library.

ISBN 978-1-108-97136-2 Paperback
ISSN 2633-3325 (online)
ISSN 2633-3317 (print)

Additional resources for this publication at www.cambridge.org/facesofcreativity

The Many Faces of Creativity

Exploring Synaesthesia through a Metaphorical Lens

Elements in Cognitive Linguistics

DOI: 10.1017/9781108974813
First published online: January 2023

Sarah Turner
Coventry University

Jeannette Littlemore
University of Birmingham

Author for correspondence: Sarah Turner, sarah.turner@coventry.ac.uk

Abstract: Creative metaphor has been of central interest to the cognitive linguistic research community in recent years. However, little is known about what propels people to use metaphor in a creative way. In this Element, the authors identify and explore some of the clues that synaesthesia may provide to help us better understand the factors that drive creativity, with a particular focus on creative metaphor. They identify the factors that seem to trigger the production of creative metaphor in synaesthetes, and explore what this can tell us about creativity in the population more generally. Their findings provide insights into the nature of creativity as it relates to metaphor, emotion and embodied experience. They argue that the production of creative metaphor arises from strong affective reactions to sensory and emotional stimuli and that there is an embodied symbiotic relationship between sensory experiences, embodiment, emotion, hyperbole, empathy, metaphor and creativity.

Keywords: metaphor, synaesthesia, creativity, emotion, sensory language

ISBNs: 9781108971362 (PB), 9781108974813 (OC)
ISSNs: 2633-3325 (online), 2633-3317 (print)

Contents

Additional resources can be accessed at www.cambridge.org/facesofcreativity

1 'Tiny Balloons Filled with Mashed Potatoes': What Is Synaesthesia, and What Has It Got to Do with Creativity and Metaphor?

1.1 What Is Synaesthesia and How Does It Relate to Creativity and Metaphor?

> I saw all my colors in spirit, before my eyes. Wild, almost crazy lines were sketched in front of me [. . .] the sound of colors is so definite that it would be hard to find anyone who would express bright yellow with bass notes or dark lake with treble.

The above words were used by the Russian artist Wassily Kandinsky in 1895 to describe the powerful visual response that he had to a performance of Wagner's Lohengrin at the Bolshoi Theatre in Moscow. For him, this was a life-changing experience that motivated him to abandon his career as a lawyer and embark on a career as an artist.

The ability to 'see' music that Kandinsky is describing here is a manifestation of a perceptual phenomenon, for which he is well known: synaesthesia. Synaesthetes (the term used to talk about people who have synaesthesia) have a particularly strong tendency to form cross-sensory associations (Simner, 2007). For synaesthetes, who constitute approximately 4 per cent of the population (Simner et al., 2006 – although estimates vary considerably across studies), the stimulation of one sensory pathway provokes involuntary stimulation of a different sensory pathway, leading people to make frequent associations between different senses (Hubbard, 2007). For example, certain sounds might be consistently associated with particular colours, textures might be associated with particular smells, tastes might be associated with particular colours, shapes or sounds, or days of the week as particular colours (Cytowic, 1989, 1994). Synaesthetes may also form connections between different facets of the same sense; for example, reading black printed graphemes may trigger the perception of different colours (Asher & Carmichael, 2013).[1] Cutting across all these types of synaesthesia is a distinction between 'associator synaesthesia', where the associations occur 'in the head', and the less common 'projector synaesthesia', where the associations are projected or superimposed onto the stimulus that triggered the synaesthetic experience. So, for example, a grapheme-colour projector synaesthete will actually see the words appearing in different colours on the page, whereas an associator synaesthete will simply see the associations in their mind's eye (van Leeuwen, 2013).

[1] The term 'synaesthesia' is something of a catchall term which incorporates different kinds of cross-sensory activation. It incorporates, for example, colour-grapheme, sequence synaesthesia, number-form synaesthesia, amongst others (Eagleman et al., 2007; Sagiv et al., 2017; Simner & Hubbard, 2013a; van Leeuwen, 2013).

The above quotation by Kandinsky is interesting. It is highly creative (music is not conventionally expressed as 'wild crazy lines'), and it draws on metaphorical associations: the idea that high treble notes are associated with light, and low bass notes with darkness. Metaphor and creativity have been of central interest to the cognitive linguistic research community in recent years, but little is known about what propels people to use them. The aim of the study presented in this book is to identify and explore some of the clues that synaesthesia may provide to help us better understand the factors that drive people to make use of metaphor and creativity. In doing so, we take up the challenge proposed by Ramachandran and Brang (2013, p. 1017), who suggest that:

> Far from being a 'fringe phenomenon' . . . synaesthesia can give us vital clues toward understanding some of the physiological mechanisms underlying some of the most elusive yet cherished aspects of the human mind.

Cytowic (2013, p. 403) suggests that 'understanding synesthetic perception might help get a handle on the neurological basis of metaphor and creativity'. Our aim is to explore how the relationships between synaesthesia, metaphor and creativity play out in written language. The study is described in detail in Sections 2–5. In this section, we discuss the relationship between synaesthesia, metaphor and creativity from a theoretical standpoint, and introduce a number of other features of synaesthesia that may also form part of the puzzle: personification, empathy, evaluation and emotion. Our reasons for including these phenomena will become clear during the course of the section.

The heightened tendency to form cross-sensory mappings in synaesthetes also extends to the descriptions that they provide of sensory experiences. We can see this in the following three sentences, all of which were produced by synaesthetes after having been asked to write about sensory experiences that they enjoyed and sensory experiences that they disliked as part of the study we report on in this book:

> *The music of Bach . . . reminds me of a large, beautiful cathedral – magnificent in its structure, beautiful in its lines, gorgeous in all the small, intimate details*
>
> *His voice melts my mind and makes me warm*
>
> *Very high pitched noises terrify me . . . they feel like thousands of red hot needles stabbing into every inch of my body over and over*

In the first example, an auditory experience (the experience of listening to Bach's music) is conveyed through a visual experience (the sight of a large, beautiful cathedral). In the second and third examples, an auditory experience is expressed by means of a tactile experience. These descriptions appear highly poetic, and are certainly not random or arbitrary. They could equally well have been produced by non-synaesthetes, but one of the questions that we explore in this book is whether synaesthetes have a heightened tendency to produce descriptions such as these, due to the neural characteristics of synaesthesia. We also explore the features of synaesthetes' language that accompany these kinds of descriptions in order to shed light on the conditions that lead to their use.

Although some of the associations that synaesthetes form may seem random and arbitrary, there has been recognition in recent years that there is a degree of systematicity to the types of associations that synaesthetes make, leading some to suggest that there are shared 'rules' underlying synaesthesia (Simner & Hubbard, 2013b). For example, when making sound-colour associations, synaesthetes tend to metaphorically map higher-pitched sounds onto lighter colours – interestingly, so do non-synaesthetes, although with less consistency (Ward et al., 2006). They also display a fairly consistent tendency to map higher-frequency words onto high-frequency chromatic colours (Simner, 2007).

Indeed, the ability to form creative cross-sensory associations is not restricted to the synaesthete population. Descriptions of one sensory experience in terms of another (as in 'a loud jacket', 'a sharp voice' or 'a soft sound') have been identified in multiple languages around the world (Speed et al., 2019; Winter, 2019). For Marks (2013) these 'synaesthetic metaphors' are a hallmark of 'weak synaesthesia', a virtually universal ability to recognise similarities between different sensory domains which gives rise to such linguistic examples. For ('strong') synaesthetes, however, these associations may be considered to an extent 'literal' in that they are experienced perceptually and go beyond language – although, as we will see later in this section, the boundary may not be as clear-cut as such a definition may lead us to assume, and even in non-synaesthetes the cross-sensory associations that are formed have been shown to have a neurophysiological basis (Ronga, 2016). However, it could be argued that synaesthetes' connections 'reflect to some extent the intuitive cross-modal correspondences of non-synaesthetes . . . synaesthesia relies not on specialised mechanisms specific only to synaesthetes, but to more universal mechanisms of general perception and cognition' (Simner, 2013, p. 160). Indeed, it has been proposed that all infants experience a form of synaesthesia due to the creation of 'exuberant connections' between neurons in the early stages of neural development, including those between areas of the brain that deal with distinct sensory systems. As the brain matures, some connections are strengthened and others 'pruned away'; some cross-sensory connections remain, but most are lost or inhibited (Maurer et al., 2013; Maurer & Mondloch, 2005). For synaesthetes, however, this 'pruning' or inhibition may not have taken place to such an extent as in non-synaesthetes. Brain imaging research has revealed that synaesthetes may exhibit stronger levels of connectivity between the areas of the brain involved in processing the senses they associate (see Rouw, 2013 for a review), or that connections between these areas are somehow disinhibited (see Mitchell, 2013).

1.2 Metaphor and Its Relationship to Synaesthesia

The fact that synaesthetes appear to exhibit high levels of neural connectivity, and have a propensity to make associations between disparate entities, has led some synaesthesia researchers to draw links between synaesthesia and metaphor. As Ramachandran and Hubbard (2005) suggest:

> just as synaesthesia involves making arbitrary links between seemingly unrelated perceptual entities like colours and numbers, metaphor involves making links between seemingly unrelated conceptual realms.

Brang and Ramachandran (2011) go on to propose:

> The overlapping region among halos of associations between two words (e.g., Juliet and the sun; both are radiant, warm, and nurturing) – the basis of metaphor – exists in all of us but is larger and stronger in synesthesia as a result of the cross-activation gene; in this formulation synesthesia is not synonymous with metaphor, but only that the gene which produces synesthesia *confers a propensity towards metaphor.*

Before exploring this link in more detail, it is worth taking a moment to consider what is meant by metaphor. Traditionally, metaphor has been described as a mechanism by which one entity is described in terms of another unrelated entity in a meaningful way, so for example, one might talk about 'understanding' in terms of 'seeing' (e.g. 'I see what you mean') or one might talk about 'morality' in terms of 'cleanliness' (e.g. 'It was a dirty business'). In recent years, however, there has been increasing awareness of the fact that metaphor does not just involve *describing* one entity in terms of another but that at times it can involve an entity being *experienced* in terms of another. In other words, metaphor is often 'experiential' (Gibbs, 2017). This applies to many of the metaphors that people employ on a day-to-day basis which are based on physical interactions with the environment. For example, strong emotions are often described in terms of warmth or heat, our experience of time is talked about in terms of space and relationships are often understood in terms of proximity (Lakoff & Johnson, 1980). Metaphors such as these are thought to underpin much of our ability to reason about abstract concepts and, for this reason, have been described as 'primary' metaphors (Grady, 1997, 2019). There is increasing evidence to suggest that metaphors involving bodily experiences such as these are, to some extent, experienced in a physical way in that they provoke sensorimotor responses in the brain (Boulenger et al., 2009). This means that, for example, a 'weighty tome', i.e. a book that literally feels heavy, will be deemed to contain more important information than one that feels light (Chandler et al., 2012; Schneider et al., 2011), and hearing texture-based metaphors such as 'a rough day' or 'a slimy person' activates the texture-selective somatosensory cortex (Lacey et al., 2012). The engagement of sensorimotor regions in response to metaphor has been found to increase when the metaphors are novel to the listener (Cacciari et al., 2011; Cardillo et al., 2012; Desai et al., 2011). These findings suggest that when we are exposed to novel metaphors that make reference to sensorimotor experiences (e.g. 'the flowers purred in the sun' (Cardillo et al., 2012)), we are more likely to experience them perceptually than when we are exposed to conventional metaphors that make reference to these experiences.

These findings support the theory of perceptual simulation (e.g. Barsalou, 1999), i.e. that hearing or reading a word triggers 'mental simulations' of perceptual or motor information that is stored in relation to that word. For example, hearing the word 'lemon' would trigger associations with the concept of 'lemon', including its taste, smell and appearance (Gray & Simner, 2015). It has been suggested that synaesthetes may experience these links in a more 'conscious' way, owing to the activation of neural connections which have been inhibited or 'pruned' in non-synaesthetes (Gray & Simner, 2015), and that these connections will then spread to other non-food-related words following phonological priming pathways until these too have tastes associated with them (Simner & Haywood, 2009). Thus, synaesthesia may be considered a 'perceptual manifestation of implicit associations that lie at the heart of embodied cognition' (Gray & Simner, 2015, p. 3).

Such a suggestion has important implications for the relationship between metaphor and synaesthesia, as it suggests a potential motivation for the connections synaesthetes make as mentioned above. Moreover, there is some evidence to suggest that core characteristics of 'primary' metaphorical mappings can also be found in the cross-sensory mappings that synaesthetes form. As we saw above, these 'primary' metaphors constitute the basic connections that exist between abstract experiences, such as 'good' and 'bad' and concrete environmental experiences such as 'light' and 'dark' (Grady, 1997). For example, when asked to associate shapes with sounds (Spector & Maurer, 2008) and pitch with different levels of lightness (Ward et al., 2006) synaesthetes and non-synaesthetes tend to produce similar metaphorical pairings. Moreover, in primary metaphors, features such as intensity, valence and extremeness are mapped from source to target in systematic ways (Barnden et al., 2003), and these principles can also be found in the cross-sensory associations that synaesthetes form involving sequences and space (Jonas & Jarick, 2013). Studies have shown that metaphorical relationships between time, number and space are motivated in the same way in both synaesthetes and non-synaesthetes but that the relationships are stronger in synaesthetes (Cohen Kadosh & Henik, 2007).

A final relationship between metaphor and synaesthesia can be found in their origins. The formation of cross-sensory metaphors is often a non-conscious, automatic (i.e. spontaneous) and 'pre-wired' process, which is observable even in prelinguistic infants (Seitz, 2005). Seitz identifies four types of metaphorical mappings that display these characteristics, namely (a) perceptual–perceptual (e.g. 'a plate of spaghetti is a bunch of worms'), (b) cross-modal (i.e. synaesthetic) (e.g. red is a 'warm' or 'hot' colour), (c) movement–movement (e.g. the similarity between a spinning top and a dancing ballerina) and (d) perceptual-affective mappings (e.g. a piece of music is 'cheerful'), arguing that, at least, in the initial stages of processing these metaphors operate largely outside of conscious awareness. Both metaphor and synaesthesia are thus pre-linguistic, automatic and involuntary (see also Cytowic, 2002).

1.3 Synaesthesia and *Creative* Metaphor

Synaesthesia brings with it benefits to creativity, which may be due to higher levels of neural connectivity, which are a significant common denominator to synaesthesia and creativity (Faust & Kenett, 2014; Kenett & Faust, 2019; Rouw & Scholte, 2007). In other words, the higher levels of neural connectivity in synaesthetes facilitate an ability to meaningful associations between disparate entities, i.e. 'associative fluency'. This is a central component of many creative thinking tasks (Mulvenna, 2013). In her survey of the literature exploring the relationship between synaesthesia and creativity, Mulvenna (2013) found extensive evidence for a synaesthetic advantage on objective measures of creative production that involve associative fluency. These included self-report measures of creativity and 'divergent thinking' tasks such as the 'Torrance' task (Torrance, 1966), where participants are invited to think of as many creative uses as possible for everyday objects. The creative advantage shown by synaesthetes also manifests in creative activities such as the production of art and music (Dailey et al., 1997). Synaesthetes are disproportionately highly represented in fields such as these (Rothen & Meier, 2010), perhaps because their abilities to form cross-sensory associations help them produce creative images, films, animations and architectural designs (Van Campen, 2010, 2013).

Associative fluency is also a key psychological process underpinning metaphor production (Littlemore & Low, 2006). At this point, it is useful to return to the three examples given at the beginning of the section:

> *The music of Bach . . . reminds me of a large, beautiful cathedral – magnificent in its structure, beautiful in its lines, gorgeous in all the small, intimate details*
>
> *His voice melts my mind and makes me warm*
>
> *Very high pitched noises terrify me . . . they feel like thousands of red hot needles stabbing into every inch of my body over and over*

We have already identified the cross-sensory connections at play in each of these examples. The fact that one experience is being described in terms of another experience with which it is not normally associated, and that this process results in a new understanding of the original experience, means that all of these examples can also be said to involve metaphor (Gibbs, 1994). In describing the music of Bach as a 'beautiful cathedral' the writer of the first sentence is creating a metaphorical mapping between the internal structure of both the music and the cathedral, which draws attention to the fact that both combine an overarching beauty with an attention to detail. In describing a man's voice in terms of warmth, the writer of the second sentence is drawing on the conventional metaphorical link between emotional attachment and heat. The writer of the third sentence is drawing on a conventional metaphorical mapping between pitch and sharpness.

These metaphors all involve a degree of novelty; we do not normally associate music with cathedrals, voices with the ability to melt our minds, or noises with red-hot needles. However, might they also be considered 'creative'? In order to answer this question, we need to consider what 'creativity' means. For an idea to be considered 'creative', it must combine *novelty* with *appropriateness* (Carter, 2015). In other words, it needs to be both original and effective (Runco & Jaeger, 2012). Creativity is therefore a two-part process; it involves a degree of free association, but there are also 'rules' governing the creative process which prevent random, meaningless combinations of ideas from being labelled as 'creative'. The kinds of associations that synaesthetes make clearly meet the first of these two criteria in that they involve novel combinations between conceptual elements which have been previously unassociated (see Carter, 2015). However, are they always *appropriate*? In the examples above, even though the descriptions are unusual, they are grounded in conventional metaphorical mappings, combining pattern-reinforcing with pattern-forming aspects of creativity (Carter, 1999). For example, while the writer of the second sentence is drawing on the conventional metaphorical link between emotional attachment and heat, he or she also develops the metaphor in a creative way to say that his voice 'melts his or her mind'. In previous work, we have shown that the creative use of metaphor often involves this kind of extension of an existing mapping (see Fuoli et al., 2021), and this kind of 'language play' has been shown to serve important communicative functions (Cook, 2000). The fact that the descriptions are grounded in existing mappings makes them accessible to non-synaesthetes. This characteristic seems to indicate a degree of audience awareness, as it enables the writers to explain their unusual experiences such that people who have not experienced them will understand. This renders them *appropriate* responses to the task. Indeed, the creative sentences produced by synaesthetes that we saw above are not wholly dissimilar to the kinds of creative cross-sensory imagery that we find in published poetry:

> And the hyacinth purple, and white, and blue,
> Which flung from its bells a sweet peal anew
> Of music so delicate, soft, and intense,
> It was felt like an odour within the sense . . .
>
> (Shelley, 1898: *The Sensitive Plant,* I, pp. 25–8)

> .. the babble of falling snowflakes . . . the scream of the reddening bud of the oak tree
>
> (Warren, 1998: *Muted Music,* p. 565)

Although the core cross-sensory associations that synaesthetes form (e.g. that 'Wednesday' is 'orange') are not necessarily intentional or goal-driven (see Ward et al., 2006), examples such as those discussed above suggest that they give rise to elaborated, novel sensory experiences, the descriptions of which can be deemed 'creative'. There is a degree of intentionality in the communication of these experiences. However, even if there had been no clear intention to be 'creative', the output could still be deemed so, as the role of intentionality in the creative process is a complex one. Many researchers highlight the role played by the unconscious mind in creative problem solving, and the fact that people 'can often sense meaningful directions of exploration in trying to solve problems, even though they might not be aware of the actual reasons underlying these choices' (Finke, 1996, p. 388). The same arguments have been applied to metaphor. As Gibbs (2017, p. 90) argues, 'many unconscious cognitive forces shape the online production and understanding of metaphors, which are simply not accessible to our conscious minds, despite our strong beliefs to the contrary'. It is therefore unlikely that there is a cut-off point between a cross-sensory metaphor that is produced as a result of a person's deliberate decision to create one, and one that is simply the result of unconscious, automatic cognitive processes. Intentionality is not therefore a necessary prerequisite for creativity.

At this point, we can make the following interim claims:

- Synaesthetic associations and metaphorical mappings are alike in that they are, to a large extent, embodied, pre-linguistic and automatic;
- The enhanced connectivity in a synaesthete's brain predisposes them to an ability to form connections between previously unrelated ideas. This is a hallmark of creativity, and also of metaphor;
- In writing about their experiences, synaesthetes seem to produce creative metaphorical mappings which draw upon embodied primary metaphorical connections.

A picture is therefore emerging of a relationship between metaphor, creativity and synaesthesia. Before introducing our study, however, there are two more areas which merit discussion due to their links with all three of these concepts: *emotion* and *empathy*.

1.4 Synaesthesia, Creative Metaphor and Emotion

Emotion has been shown to play a key role in inducing synaesthetic associations (Callejas & Lupiáñez, 2013), and synaesthetes often report strong emotional reactions to the cross-sensory associations that they form (Cytowic & Eagleman, 2009). For example, they may derive pleasure from the associations that they form, but they experience strong negative emotional reactions to pairings that they perceive to be 'incorrect', such as when numbers are printed in the 'wrong' colour (Callejas & Lupiáñez, 2013; Safran & Sanda, 2015). This can be accounted for by the fact that synaesthetes have been found to exhibit hyper-connectivity between the amygdala (which is involved in the processing of emotions) and the sensory cortex (which is involved in the processing of sensory stimuli) (Ramachandran & Hubbard, 2005). In other words, the fact that the sensory cortex is strongly connected to the amygdala suggests that emotion may play a role in the cross-sensory associations that synaesthetes form. In addition to this, people with auditory-visual synaesthesia show significantly more brain activation in the inferior parietal cortex during sound perception, than non-synaesthetes. Crucially, this part of the brain is responsible for multi-modal integration, the perception of emotions and the interpretation of sensory information (Neufeld et al., 2012).

Emotions can also play a part in the synaesthetic associations themselves. For example, some synaesthetes report unpleasant events in their lives being associated with a particular colour (Safran & Sanda, 2015), particular emotions may also trigger colour associations and words with particularly emotional connotations may be more likely to elicit synaesthetic responses (Ward, 2004).

Emotions can also be the synaesthetic response to particular stimuli, as in the case of 'tactile-emotion' synaesthesia in which particular textures elicit emotional responses (Ramachandran & Brang, 2008).

Emotion is also heavily implicated in the production of cross-sensory metaphor in the non-synaesthete population (Marks, 2013). Marks draws on ideas from embodied cognition to explain this link, arguing that metaphorical cross-sensory mappings in the non-synaesthete population emerge from 'a nexus of affective and motor as well as perceptual responses to sensory stimulation' (Marks, 2013, p. 779). These include 'physiognomic perception', which he describes as 'the relatively undifferentiated affective and expressive qualities of perceptual experience, as when we see a willow tree as "sad"' (Marks, 2013, p. 779). In other words, when we witness an object, we sometimes cannot help but experience an emotional response to it, and this response sometimes results in empathy. Indeed, evidence for a strong link between emotion and metaphor more generally can be found in neuroimaging studies (Citron & Goldberg, 2014; Citron & Zervos, 2018) which demonstrate that even conventional metaphorical sentences are more emotionally evocative than their literal counterparts. Affect and involvement have been shown to be a driving force in the production of metaphor (Foolen, 2012), and *personal* emotional experiences have been found to lead people to produce creative metaphor (Fainsilber & Ortony, 1987). People have been found to use more metaphor, particularly creative metaphor, when talking about personal emotional experiences (Williams-Whitney et al., 1992), and it appears to be the first-hand experience of these emotions which provides the motivation for creative metaphor production (MacCormac, 1986). Other studies have shown that, even in non-synaesthetes, one of the main things that drive people to make metaphorical connections between colours, patterns and music is emotion (Lindborg & Friberg, 2015; Palmer et al., 2013).

Furthermore, the instruction to think explicitly about how one might react in an emotional way to an imagined experience has been shown to trigger associative fluency, which in turn leads to the production of creative metaphor (Lubart & Getz, 1997). Lubart and Getz argue that experiencing an emotional reaction to a given concept or experience can help trigger a resonating endocept, whose attachment to the original concept or experience then becomes active in working memory. They argue that:

> at this point, the raw materials for a metaphor are present: a target concept and a source concept that is emotionally related to the problem but possibly cognitively distant. Metaphor generation can proceed through the exploration, transformation, and mapping between the two concepts and their domains. We hypothesize that a metaphor formed through this emotion-based process

> possesses higher creative potential than a metaphor formed through a purely cognitive process because of the individualized nature of endocepts.
> (Lubart & Getz, 1997, p. 292)

They illustrated this theory by having a group of business students focus consciously on the emotional experiences that they associated with being in an elevator, and then asked them to generate metaphorical associations that an elevator might have. This led to a number of associations, including a metaphor that was produced by one student, where being in an elevator was seen as being like an animal in a cage. The student then went on to reason that, like animals, people in an elevator may perceive their 'cage' to be boring because the scenery is unchanging. One idea resulting from this metaphor was to change the displays (e.g., posters) on the walls of elevators. Another insight from the zoo-cage metaphor was that people may find elevators uninviting because they lack features of their natural habitat; elevators could thus be improved by furnishing them in the style of a person's living room. Thus, in this case, the instruction to access one's emotional responses to the feeling of being in an elevator triggered the generation of an apt, creative metaphor along with its entailments.

Emotion has been shown to be a key driver in the creative process more generally (Russ, 2013), and the use of multisensory imagery has been shown to be a key strategy that non-synaesthetes employ when invited to express their emotions creatively through the media of poetry and art, with embarrassment being found to provoke the use of tactile imagery, and romantic or sensual emotions provoking the use of olfactory and taste sensory images (Shaw, 2008). This links to more general research showing that when people have negative emotional experiences, this drives the production of creative outputs (e.g. Bastian, 2017; Schubert, 1996), and in particular creative metaphor (Fainsilber & Ortony, 1987; Littlemore et al., forthcoming b; Winner, 2018). This may be a reflection of the so-called 'negativity bias' which has been observed in the general population (Jing-Schmidt, 2007). People have been found to give greater weight to negative entities, which means that they are more likely to pay attention to negative entities and events, and to remember them (Rozin & Royzman, 2001). Negative experiences are therefore more vivid, and according to the vividness hypothesis (Fainsilber & Ortony, 1987), more vivid experiences trigger more creative metaphor use. Thus, the desire to produce creative metaphor may emanate in part from the need to share negative emotional experiences.

1.4.1 Positive and Negative Evaluation

Closely linked to the role played by emotion in triggering cross-sensory metaphorical connections is the role played by positive and negative evaluation.

Indeed, the linguistic expression of emotion, known as *affect*, is generally considered as an integral part of the broader phenomenon of evaluation. Within Martin and White's (2005) appraisal framework, affect is considered as the most basic type of evaluative meaning, with other forms of evaluation representing 'institutionalised' emotions. The use of metaphor has long been associated with the need to express evaluation (Semino, 2008), and in their study of the interaction between metaphor and evaluation in film reviews, Fuoli et al. (2021) found that metaphors played an important evaluative role. Furthermore, creative metaphors were significantly more likely to perform an evaluative function than conventional metaphors, reminiscent of the link between creativity and emotion discussed in the previous section.

We saw above that a link has been posited between emotion and the use of cross-sensory metaphor by non-synaesthetes. Similarly, there is evidence to suggest a potential role of affect and evaluation in use of cross-sensory metaphor (see Winter, 2019, p. 227). In his corpus-based study of cross-sensory metaphor, Winter (2019, pp. 227–30) found that the more emotionally valenced an adjective is, the more likely it is used in a cross-modal expression, i.e. a synesthetic metaphor. For example, adjective–noun combinations such as 'sweet music' were found to be more frequent than combinations such as 'palatable music' because 'sweet' is more valenced than 'palatable'.

The directional value of the evaluation is also an important factor to consider when exploring the extent to which emotional experience triggers creative cross-sensory metaphor. It has been shown that synaesthetic metaphors involving adjectives (e.g., 'brown smell') tend to evoke more negative interpretations than nominal metaphors (e.g. 'my job is a jail') or predicative metaphors (e.g. 'he shot down all my arguments') (Sakamoto & Utsumi, 2014). Moreover, Sakamoto and Utsumi found that the more creative the metaphor, the more likely it was to evoke negative meanings. In their study of the ways in which people use metaphor to describe positive and negative workplace experiences, Littlemore et al. (forthcoming b) found that creative metaphor was more likely to perform *negative* evaluation than conventional metaphor. This last finding differs from previous work on (for example) the use of metaphor in film reviews, which did not show such a clear distinction (Fuoli et al., 2021). Littlemore et al. argue that it can be accounted for by the fact that in their study participants are talking about their own *personal* experiences, and it is the personal nature of the experiences that appears to drive the relationship between creativity and negativity, at least in part.

Bringing these two sections together, we see links between emotional experiences and a desire to evaluate experiences, and the production of (creative) metaphor. When investigating cross-sensory, synaesthetic metaphor specifically, a similar relationship has been established between emotion, evaluation and the use of such metaphors. This connection may be stronger in synaesthetes than in non-synaesthetes, but it is present in both populations. Previous research has also indicated a potential link between negative evaluation, or negative emotions, and the use of (creative) metaphor.

1.5 Synaesthesia, Personification and Empathy

An important characteristic that has been found to be strongly associated with synaesthesia is the tendency to personify objects (Sobczak-Edmans & Sagiv, 2013). This characteristic, which is found in approximately 33 per cent of the synaesthete population (Amin et al., 2011), is automatic and involuntary (Simner & Holenstein, 2007), and can be viewed as a kind of metaphor as it involves perceiving an object or entity in terms of something that it is not (i.e. a human). The personification of stimuli allows social and affective characteristics to be attributed to them (Sobczak-Edmans & Sagiv, 2013). For example, a synaesthete might attribute personality traits to linguistic inducers such as graphemes, an example of 'ordinal linguistic personification' (OLP) (Simner & Holenstein, 2007, p. 694). Amin et al. (2011) report that when synaesthetes attribute human characteristics to inducers such as these, they often refer to 'human-style' relationships between them, so inanimate objects might be 'friends', 'enemies', members of the same social group and so on. Smilek et al. (2007) classified the social and affective characteristics that synaesthetes attribute to stimuli into four types: physical (gender, physical appearance); personal (cognitive ability, personality, mental states, moods, inclinations); relations (emotive and behavioural responses to other stimuli) and social role (occupation, familial and non-familial relationships).

While there is some controversy over the extent to which this 'grapheme-personality synaesthesia' is indeed synaesthesia as it does not involve a cross-modal perceptual experience, many definitions of synaesthesia have now been broadened to include non-sensory elements (such as personality) (Sagiv et al., 2017). Indeed, the mechanisms underlying the personification have been shown to be reminiscent of the more 'prototypical' synaesthetic connections described earlier, as they have been attributed to the hyper-connectivity that is a characteristic of a synaesthete's brain. It has been postulated that the personification of linguistic inducers is caused by the heightened levels of 'cross-talk' between the left inferior parietal lobe (which is responsible for sequencing) and 'social brain' regions that are responsible for personality trait attribution (such as the amygdala and the somatosensory cortex) (Simner & Hubbard, 2006).

The tendency to personify objects can also be found in the general population, particularly in infancy (Sagiv et al., 2017; Sobczak-Edmans & Sagiv, 2013). According to the neonatal synaesthesia hypothesis (Maurer & Mondloch, 2005), all newborn babies experience synaesthesia, and the tendency to personify inanimate objects has also been attested in early infancy (Piaget, 2002). Piaget argues that this form of thinking, which usually recedes in adulthood (although see Degani & Onysko, 2021), provides a mechanism for constructing reality with the self as the model. The brain areas associated with self-referential processing have also been found to be implicated in animistic thinking, including personification (Sagiv et al., 2017; Sobczak-Edmans & Sagiv, 2013), and Amin et al. (2011) attribute the synaesthete's heightened use of personification to heightened activation of the precuneus, which is associated with self-referential processing. Therefore, it may be reasonable to suggest that types of synaesthesia which involve personification are a 'residual expression of childhood animism' (Sobczak-Edmans & Sagiv, 2013, p. 235), just as the more sense-based forms of synaesthesia may be a residual expression of the abundant neural connections present in early infancy. Interestingly, as with other kinds of synaesthetic connections, the principles underpinning the ways in which inanimate objects are personified have been found to be similar in synaesthetes and non-synaesthetes (Sobczak-Edmans & Sagiv, 2013). For example, when asked what kind of personalities they would attribute to letters of the alphabet, both synaesthetes and non-synaesthetes attributed positive personal characteristics to frequently used letters and negative personal characteristics to less frequently used letters.

Once an inanimate object has been personified, many synaesthetes then go on to empathise with the object in some way, for example by expressing sympathy for an object that is excluded from the group (Amin et al., 2011). This has led some researchers to posit a relationship between synaesthesia and empathy levels, with mixed results. In one study of empathy levels in personifying synaesthetes, some participants were indeed found to exhibit higher levels of empathy than average, whereas others scored considerably lower (Amin et al., 2011). This finding led the researchers to suggest two different developmental routes to grapheme personification, 'one representing an exaggeration or extension of normal processes (from the domain of human interaction to other domains), while the other could represent impaired criteria for personification, or sensitivity to the "wrong" cues' (Amin et al., 2011, p. 277). However, mirror-touch synaesthesia, in which observing touch evokes a conscious sensation on the observer's own body (e.g. Blakemore et al., 2005) entails 'self-other blurring' (Maister et al., 2013), and has been linked with heightened emotional empathy and ability to read facial expressions of emotion (Banissy & Ward, 2007; Ward et al., 2018).

The existence of mirror-touch synaesthesia provides further evidence for the link between synaesthesia and embodied cognition. In Section 3, we introduced the theory of embodied cognition, noting that some researchers have suggested that synaesthetes consciously experience embodied links between perceptions and words – that synaesthesia is therefore a case of 'disinhibited embodiment' (Gray & Simner, 2015, p. 1). In synaesthetes and non-synaesthetes alike, mirror neurons allow for understanding, imitation and prediction of the behaviour of those around us by *simulating* these actions. However, when watching an action leads to a physical sensation related to that action (as in the case of mirror-touch synaesthesia), it may be that this is due to the synaesthete consciously experiencing this embodied simulation that is found in the population as a whole (Banissy & Ward, 2007; Gray & Simner, 2015). Banissy and Ward's (2007) finding that mirror-touch synaesthetes exhibited higher levels of emotional empathy could also indicate that mirror neurons have a role to play in empathy.

At this point, we can suggest a potential role for *empathy* in the overall picture we have built up over this section. The studies introduced here allow us to propose potential links between synaesthesia, creativity, metaphor and empathy. It is these links that we aim to explore in more depth over the course of this book.

1.6 Bringing It All Together: Our Study

We have seen that synaesthesia, metaphor and creativity are interlinked, and that emotion and evaluation can modulate these relationships. We have also seen that personification, as well as being a type of metaphor in itself, is an important feature of many synaesthetes' connections. Specifically, we have seen that: (a) synaesthetes display higher levels of creativity than the general population; (b) the cross-sensory associations that synaesthetes make appear to be metaphorically motivated, and may also be considered creative; (c) the neurological architecture of the synaesthete is characterised by higher levels of connectivity between parts of the brain that are responsible for sensory awareness, emotion and self-referential processing; (d) synaesthetes' cross-sensory associations are often associated with particularly high levels of emotion, personification and empathy, and (e) emotion and evaluation are closely linked and the need to express emotional experiences or evaluation has been found to drive the production of (creative) metaphor. These attested links between synaesthesia, associative fluency and emotion provide support for the idea that it is the strong, emotional responses to sensory experiences that synaesthetes have that drive their creative use of metaphor.

It may be useful to explore the relationship between these characteristics in order to better understand the role that they play in metaphorical creativity and potentially in creativity more generally. As we saw at the beginning of this section, Ramachandran and Brang (2013, p. 1017) suggest that:

> Far from being a 'fringe phenomenon' . . . synaesthesia can give us vital clues toward understanding some of the physiological mechanisms underlying some of the most elusive yet cherished aspects of the human mind.

We take up their challenge by conducting an in-depth examination of what 'looks like' creative metaphor, and identifying features that appear to be associated with this style of thinking. By doing so, we hope to shed light on the factors that seem to trigger the production of creative metaphor in synaesthetes and, by extension, in the population more generally. A key part of this enquiry involves identifying key characteristics of synaesthetes' descriptions of positive and negative sensory experiences, and exploring the ways in which they differ from descriptions provided by non-synaesthetes. We explore similarities and differences between people with and without synaesthesia in terms of (a) their propensity to produce cross-sensory creative metaphor when describing positive and negative sensory experiences, (b) the clusters of features that accompany or trigger the production of cross-sensory creative metaphor, and (c) the associations they provide in response to emotion words. Our overall aim is to establish the extent to which the responses provided by synaesthetes resemble those made by non-synaesthetes in both qualitative and quantitative terms.

We explore the metaphorical nature of the associations that synaesthetes make, compare their propensity to make such associations with that of non-synaesthetes and identify the factors that co-occur with, or seem to give rise to, these kinds of associations, with a particular focus on evaluation, empathy and personification. We seek to establish the extent to which the associations that are produced by synaesthetes involve metaphor, whether or not synaesthetes form creative metaphorical mappings more often than the general population, and if so, what (if anything) synaesthesia might tell us anything about associative fluency and metaphorical creativity. To put it another way, our aim is to conduct an in-depth examination of a style of thinking that 'looks like' creative metaphor, to identify features that appear to be associated with this style of thinking in order to better understand the nature of metaphorical creativity.

Our research questions are therefore as follows:

1. How do the responses of synaesthetes and non-synaesthetes differ from one another:
   a. When asked to write critical descriptions of positive and negative sensory experiences?
   b. When asked what words they associate with emotion words?

2. What do these differences reveal about the relationship between metaphor, creativity and emotion?

In order to answer these questions, we compare and contrast the responses provided by the synaesthetes and non-synaesthetes in terms of:

- The range and types of cross-sensory associations that are made
- The extent to which they produce (creative cross-sensory) metaphor
- References to personification, empathy, emotion and other features emerging from the data
- The extent to which and the ways in which all of the above interact with one another

Our hypotheses are that in comparison with non-synaesthetes, synaesthetes will make use of a wider range of cross-sensory associations, and make more use of cross-sensory associations, personification, empathy and emotion. We also hypothesise that that there will be more inter-relationships between these response types in the synaesthete population than in the non-synaesthete population due to the higher levels of neural connectivity discussed in this section. The study also has an exploratory element in that we do not restrict ourselves to these response types and aim to identify, through a maximally inclusive iterative coding procedure, other response types that have not been identified in the literature.

In the remaining sections, we outline the methodology used in the study and present the findings. In Sections 2 and 3, we describe the methodology (Section 2) and discuss the findings (Section 3) from the first part of our study, in which we investigated the responses provided by synaesthetes and non-synaesthetes when asked to describe something they liked and something they did not like to see, hear, taste, smell and touch. In Section 4, we present the methodology and discuss the findings from the second part of our study in which we explored the responses that our participants produced when presented with emotion words. In Section 5, we provide a brief conclusion and consider the implications of our findings for our understandings of synaesthesia, metaphor and creativity.

2 'Those Cookies Tasted of Regret . . . ': How We Investigated Evaluative Descriptions of Sensory Experiences

2.1 Introduction

The aim of the study presented in this book is to identify and explore some of the clues that synaesthesia may provide to help us better understand creativity, or, more specifically, creative metaphor. In order to do this, we compare the responses that synaesthetes and non-synaesthetes provide to sensory and emotive prompts.

Through the use of an online survey, developed using and hosted on the Qualtrics platform, we asked a group of people who identified as synaesthetes and a group of people who did not identify as synaesthetes to participate in two tasks in which they responded to prompts involving sensory experiences and emotion words. For the sake of brevity, the two groups are labelled 'synaesthetes' and 'non-synaesthetes', although we acknowledge that the distinction is by no means as clear-cut. The questionnaire is shown in **Figure A1** in the additional resources.

2.2 Participants

All participants were recruited online. Synaesthete participants (N=20) were recruited through the UK Synaesthesia Association (who included a link to our study in their member's newsletter[2]), the Synesthesia List[3] and the synaesthesia subreddit.[4] The URL was also shared on Twitter, using the hashtags #synesthesia, #synaesthesia and the URL link was shared to synaesthesia-related groups on Facebook. The non-synaesthetes (N=20) were recruited online through social media via an advertisement. The link was open for twelve weeks in total. Participants in the non-synaesthete group were advised that if they had synaesthesia they should not complete the questionnaire. This recruitment procedure meant that one of our groups of participants had self-reported a strong tendency to form cross-sensory associations, and the other group had not.

In the advertisement, potential participants were told that the research would involve a series of short writing tasks, but no mention was made of metaphor or creativity, as this may have led to response bias (see e.g. Furnham, 1986). The Participant Information Sheet indicated that the purpose of the study was to 'investigate the link between language and synaesthesia'. All participants were native-level speakers of English and over eighteen years of age. The study was granted ethical approval by the University of Birmingham. The demographic breakdown of our participants (age and gender) is shown in **Table A1** in the additional resources.

Synaesthete participants were asked what kind(s) of synaesthesia they had and whether they had associator or projector synaesthesia. Seventeen reported experiencing associator synaesthesia, one reported experiencing projector synaesthesia and two reported experiencing both types of synaesthesia. Participants reported a range of types of association, with most participants reporting more than one

[2] www.uksynaesthesia.com/index.html. [3] www.daysyn.com/Synesthesia-List.html.
[4] www.reddit.com/r/Synesthesia/.

type. The types of synaesthetic association reported are shown in **Table A2** in the additional resources.

This research design is not without its risks. Firstly, the participants in the 'synaesthete' group may have contained a number of 'false positives', i.e. individuals who would not be classified as having synaesthesia as measured by standard tests (see Mulvenna, 2013). However, to the best of our knowledge standard tests for synaethaesia, such as the 'Test of Genuineness' (Asher et al., 2006), focus exclusively on colour synaesthesia (Carmichael et al., 2015) and in our study we were interested in a wider range of synaesthetic experiences. The main focus of our study was on the tendency to make cross-sensory associations and characteristics that appear to accompany that tendency.

Secondly, the self-selecting nature of this group may have meant that they saw the task as an opportunity to 'perform' their identity as synaesthetes. This may have led to them providing more detailed responses or responses that demonstrate features that they thought we might be looking for in the project. In order to mitigate this, as we saw above we made no mention of metaphor or creativity in the recruitment or in the instructions for participants.

2.3 Procedure

In the first task, participants were asked to identify and describe something that they did and did not like to see, hear, taste, smell and feel. There was no word limit or time limit for this task. We (the two authors) coded their free-text responses for features that have been observed in the literature (e.g. personification, empathy, references to emotion, and metaphor) as well as other features that emerged from our analysis. We saw in Section 1.2 that synaesthetes have been found to perform better than non-synaesthetes in divergent thinking tests, which are thought to be measures of creativity. However, these tests are largely decontextualised and generally do not require participants to discuss real-world experiences or to provide reasons for their responses. To the best of our knowledge, no studies to date have looked at metaphorical creativity when synaesthetes and non-synaesthetes are performing free-writing tasks in which they are invited to provide personal responses to sensory experiences. Moreover, given the apparent importance of emotion, personification and empathy in synaesthetic responses to stimuli, we were interested in comparing their reactions to phenomena that they did and did not like. As we saw above, there is evidence to suggest that people are particularly likely to produce creative metaphor when reacting in an emotional way to a stimulus (Lubart & Getz, 1997), and this effect is intensified when they are responding to *negative* emotional experiences (Fainsilber & Ortony, 1987; Winner, 2018). We were interested in investigating whether this valence extends to the synaesthete population, as they have been found to express strong positive and negative emotional reactions to sensory experiences.

The second task was a word association task in which we investigated their responses to the six 'basic' emotion words: 'happiness', 'sadness', 'fear', 'anger', 'surprise' and 'disgust' (Ekman, 1992). Whereas in the first task, we hoped to elicit personal, potentially emotional responses to external entities, in this task we sought to investigate how synaesthetes and non-synaesthetes *respond* to emotional language by identifying what kinds of things they associate with it. Again, we coded their responses for features that have been identified in the literature on synaesthesia (e.g. colours, letters of the alphabet, physical sensations, novelty) as well as other features that emerged in our analysis of the data (e.g. scenarios, actions, physical objects).

In both tasks, we identified the ways in which the synaesthetes and the non-synaesthetes differed from one another in terms of their response patterns, and examined the different ways in which different types of response interacted with one another in both populations in order to better characterise the response patterns exhibited by the synaesthetes. Our hypothesis was that these response patterns would provide insights into the mechanisms underlying synaesthetes' purported higher propensity towards the production of creative metaphor.

In this section, our focus is on the first task. We describe the methodology, outline the characteristics of the corpus and introduce the coding scheme that was used to annotate it.

2.4 Characteristics of the Corpus

Each participant produced a total of 10 written responses (a positive and a negative response for each of the five senses), resulting in a total of 400 written responses (N=40 participants x 10 responses each). These written responses resulted in a corpus made up of 15,151 words for the synaesthete responses and 6,970 words for the non-synaesthete responses.[5] In **Table A3** in the additional resources we provide a breakdown of the corpus, showing the number of words that were used to talk about each of the senses in positive or negative terms.

It is interesting to note that the synaesthetes wrote significantly more than the non-synaesthetes. This may be because the synaesthetes' sensory experiences are to a certain extent 'richer' than those of their non-synaesthete counterparts as not only do they experience the stimulus through the primary sense, they also have access to the associations this stimulus triggers. As we saw in Section 1, synaesthesia may also entail a greater emotional engagement with the experience

[5] Unfortunately, we are not able to share the complete corpus as we did not obtain permission from the participants to share their submissions in their entirety.

(e.g. Cytowic & Eagleman, 2009). They also demonstrate higher performance in a variety of memory tasks (see Meier & Rothen, 2013 for a review). It has been suggested that this is due to the increased richness of their experience; because synaesthetes encode additional features into their memory (e.g. colour may be associated with numbers), they can take advantage of a wider range of retrieval cues (Rothen et al., 2020) which may allow them to recall richer, more emotional experiences in greater detail. Although the longer productions by the synaesthetes may partly be explained by the fact that the synaesthetes' sensory experiences may have been richer than those of the non-synaesthetes, they may also have been explained by the fact that they may have had a correspondingly strong urge to communicate these rich experiences. The longer responses may also reflect the characteristics of the sample of synaesthetes used in our study. The fact that they were recruited through a synaesthesia forum suggests that they have strong identities as synaesthetes and that they may have viewed the activity as an opportunity to express these identities.

There was also a difference in behaviour relating to the two groups' descriptions of positive and negative sensory experiences. Whilst both groups said more about positive sensory experiences than negative sensory experiences, the difference was noticeably more marked in the synaesthetes than in the non-synaesthetes. We also found that the synaesthetes produced more words in response to positive prompts for sight, sound, smell and touch and more words in response to negative prompts for taste. Non-synaesthetes produced more words in response to positive prompts for sight, sound and smell, and more words for negative prompts for taste and touch. These findings suggest that the 'negativity bias' discussed in Section 1 may be less marked in synaesthetes than in non-synaesthetes, possibly reflecting the levels of 'enjoyment' that synaesthetes sometimes report when making cross-sensory associations.

2.5 Coding Procedure and Scheme

Both authors coded the entire dataset together and engaged in extensive, in-depth discussion in order to establish the coding categories. The decision to work together on the entire dataset rather than taking a section each and comparing was due to the fact that we were not working exclusively with a priori categories. A major part of the research endeavour involved developing the scheme either through identifying new categories or by delineating categories that reflected or built on ideas that had been suggested in the literature on synaesthesia. This involved making multiple passes of the data and discussing the emerging structure of the scheme as the categories became apparent.

Responses were first coded according to the sense and valence of the sensory experience that was being described (e.g. responses to 'write about something you like to hear' were coded as 'sound' and 'positive'). Following this, a coding scheme was developed to identify the types of responses that were provided. This scheme was first informed by previous research into creativity and synaesthesia as introduced in the literature review, and then honed through an iterative process. It had three overarching groups of categories: *response sense*, to identify the senses activated in the responses; *response type*, to identify the broad types of response being given, e.g. emotional, empathic, etc.; and *'metaphorical' theme*. A single response could be coded into more than one category and more than one group.

2.5.1 Coding for Response Senses

The 'response sense' coding level was used to identify which of the five senses (sight, hearing, touch, smell and taste) were being activated in the responses. Although the categorisation of the range of human sensory experiences in to these five senses is a somewhat artificial idea (Serres, 2008; Winter, 2019), the five-sense model was adopted for practical purposes in this study to allow for an exploration of the extent to which the two populations varied in terms of the breadth of sensory experiences that they drew on. These categories were reasonably easy to identify. By way of illustration, here is an example from a synaesthete's response to what they did not like to hear:

> *I absolutely hate most loud noises. The sound of vacuums, drills, leaf blowers, yelling/screaming/arguing, vomiting, noisy classrooms, and crying are some of the sounds I hate the most. It doesn't help that most of these sounds make me see colors I don't like looking at as much. I like all colors, but I'm more of a fan of cool colors (greens, blues, purples) than warm colors (reds, oranges, yellows). Vacuums make me see so much red it's actually a little uncomfortable. Vomiting is beige.*

Because this participant explains their dislike of these sounds by referring back to the colours these sounds make them see, this example was coded as 'response sense – sight'.

2.5.2 Coding for Response Types

The coding for response types necessitated the development of a bespoke coding scheme, which was developed through an iterative process. Some coding categories were identified from the outset, based on our reading of the literature on synaesthesia, and our interest in the role played by metaphor in synaesthetic 'creativity'. These were: 'metaphor', 'emotional effects', 'personification', 'empathy and identification', and 'literal explanations and associations'. The other categories emerged as we analysed the data. These were 'cognitive effects', 'value judgements', 'physical effects' and 'hyperbole'. These categories were of particular interest as they emerged from our data and were not predicted by our review of the literature. They provided additional insights into the features that accompany, and possibly drive, the production of creative output – specifically metaphorical cross-sensory mappings.

The coding scheme is as follows:

1. Emotional effects

This category was used in cases where participants included explanations of particular emotional effects to the objects or experiences being described. For example:

> *Eating noises, particularly squishy ones. They make me feel* ***anxious and disgusted****.*
>
> *Generally the colour yellow I find* ***cheers me up****, e.g. lots of daffodils bunched together.*
>
> *Very high-pitched noises.* ***These terrify me.*** *If any of my skin is left uncovered when I hear these sounds, I NEED it to be covered immediately.*

Here the participants are talking about how the sensory experiences they are describing make them feel anxious, cheerful or terrified.

2. Cognitive effects

This category was used in cases where participants were describing an object or experience which had an effect on the way they thought. For example:

> *I don't like when people talk in the background when I do things because* ***I can't help but focus on what they say as a result of the shapes being present in the back of my mind****.*
>
> *. . . metal being banged against metal, (pots and pans, for example). These sort of 'stun' me. My body goes numb, yet tingly, my vision goes blurry, and* ***thoughts become . . . Odd. I'll think in non-human languages, or shapes, or an amalgamation of multiple things at once****.*

In the first example, the participant comments that people talking in the background create shapes in their mind that prevents them from concentrating on the task at hand. In the second example, the participant comments that when they hear metal being banged against metal, their thoughts become 'odd'. In both cases, the sensory stimulus leads to changes or disruptions to their thinking patterns, i.e. 'cognitive effects'.

3. Physical effects

This category was used for examples where participants described having a physical, bodily response to the sensory object or experience being described. In the first of the following examples, the experience gives the participant a headache and in the second example, it makes them feel physically sick.

> *I really dislike not having lyrics to songs. I feel the same about death metal where lyrics are not discernible.* ***It gives me a headache and makes me uncomfortable.***
>
> *Marmite makes me* ***heave****.*

4. Personification

This category was used in cases where the sensory experience under discussion was attributed some kind of human characteristic. Although strictly speaking, personification is most appropriately viewed as a kind of metaphor, the prevalence of this feature in the literature on synaesthesia led us to include it as a separate category in its own right. Examples of personification included:

> *The waves seem* ***angry*** *and I do not trust them*
>
> *Lemons.* ***Lemons need to chill out.***
>
> *Water which is flavored, but only slightly. What are you? Are you water or are you flavored water?* ***Pick something!***

Here, waves, lemons and water are being given human characteristics and, in the latter two cases, a degree of agency: lemons need to 'chill out' and flavoured water needs to 'make up its mind about what it wants to be'.

5. Empathy

We introduced research that indicated a link between synaesthesia and heightened or altered levels of empathy in Section 1, and postulated a potential role for empathy in the creative process. In order to investigate the types of empathy provoked and their relationship to metaphor, we therefore included 'empathy' as a response category. It was used in cases where participants expressed a sense of empathy or identification with the object or experience under discussion. In some cases it was applied to a person, as in the following example, where the participant describes feeling empathy with people who are in pain:

> *I don't like to . . . see other people in pain because* ***it triggers pain in me****.*

However, in other cases, empathy was expressed towards a concept or physical object which had been personified, as in the following example, where the participant identifies with the colour purple:

Purple's ***personality*** *is very compatible with mine*

In other cases the object was not personified; rather, the participant put themselves in the place of the inanimate object, as in the following example:

I enjoy pretty much all lines and shapes. I can literally feel the outline of whatever I stare at, so much so that it's almost as if I become the shape itself. This makes me feel . . . Different. Like I'm not myself anymore. The reason this is enjoyable is that it helps to 'empathize' with things that most people probably wouldn't even know you could empathize with; yellow street-lines, beehives, computer monitors, etc . . . (I use empathize in a way similar to, but not exactly like its actual definition. Rather, it is closer to a feeling of 'complete understanding' of that one object).

All three kinds of cases were coded as 'empathy' and we did not distinguish between them.

6. Value judgements

This category was used for examples where participants expressed some form of judgement as to how something should or should not be, often with a moral or ethical component or a sense that there is a correct or an incorrect state of being. For example:

I don't like the smell of burning leaves. It's close to campfire smell (which is pleasant) but it has a weird sour overtone that just makes it smell ***wrong***.

Stronger flavours just seem more ***worthwhile***.

The respondent in the first example comments that the sour overtone of the campfire smell is somehow 'wrong', and the participant in the second example comments that stronger flavours as somehow more 'worthwhile'. In both cases, judgements are being made about what is 'right' or 'worthwhile' and what is 'wrong'. The implication is that there is something intrinsically bad about sour smells and something intrinsically good about strong flavours. No reasons are offered for these responses; the judgements are highly subjective.

7. 'Hyperbole'

We saw in Section 1 that synaesthetes sometimes experience extreme reactions to sensory experiences, and that these reactions can be positive or negative. In order to explore whether, and if so how, the responses provided by the synaesthetes differed from those of the non-synaesthetes in terms of extremeness, we needed a measure that would capture this characteristic. Unfortunately, 'extremeness' is not a concept that is easy to capture objectively. The nearest concept that one can capture is 'hyperbole', which involves 'amplification or attenuation used to express emotion and not to be taken literally' (Norrick, 2004, p. 1728). The term 'hyperbole' captures the combination of 'amplification' and 'improbability' that characterised some of the responses. However, we are somewhat uncomfortable using the term 'hyperbole' at face value for these data, as in some cases, for the synaesthetes in particular, what they are describing is not intended to be understood as any kind of exaggeration. We therefore use the term in inverted commas throughout and recognise the subjectivity of this category.

The 'hyperbole' category was used in cases where the participant provided an amplified and improbable description of the sensory experience. We can see this in the following examples:

> *Every time I see overly-long fingernails, I feel a scratching/ peeling feeling in my nails,* ***as if they're being ripped off****.*
>
> *Really, really loud rock music . . . Physical pain plus* ***obliteration of any sort of thinking or feeling*** *is why I hate it.*
>
> *They* ***wear a hole*** *in your mind.*

As we can see in these examples, responses that were coded as 'hyperbole' sometimes also involved metaphor. This is unsurprising, given that hyperbole and metaphor often overlap (e.g. Barnden, 2018, 2020).

8. Literal Explanations and Associations

This category was used in cases where participants were explaining their like or dislike of a particular object or experience by referring in a very literal way to the meaning of the stimulus or drawing on the memories or associations it evokes. For example:

> *I don't like to hear the noise made by the rotor blades on Chinook helicopter . . . If I hear it where I live, it means severely injured soldiers are being taken to hospital.*
>
> *Petunias. It reminds me of a place where we used to go on holiday, where there were lots growing by the main footpath.*

In both cases, there is a clear, literal explanation for their enjoyment or dislike of the object.

2.5.3 Coding for Metaphor

Although strictly speaking a 'response type', we include metaphor here as a distinct category as it forms the main focus of this book. This category was used in cases where a participant produced a response that involved describing one experience in terms of another. We did not seek to identify metaphor at the level of the lexical unit (Pragglejaz, 2007), rather at the level of the metaphorical 'experience' as our aim was to establish the number of different metaphorical experiences that the participants reported. We did not distinguish between similes and metaphors; we followed Cameron and Deignan (2003) in viewing words such as 'like', 'kind of' and 'sort of', and 'as (if)' as 'tuning devices' that prepare the reader for the use of metaphor. For example, the response 'I hate hearing very loud clear high notes because the sounds look like white jagged walls and it gets too overwhelming' was coded as a single metaphorical experience as the participant is describing a single metaphorical scene in which the sounds are experienced as 'white jagged walls' and deems this experience 'overwhelming'. Similarly, 'I think sawdust smells clean, bright, fresh, and slightly tangy' was coded as a single metaphorical experience as it reports a unified metaphorical experience of sawdust, and the four adjectives work together to express this single, unified experience. The majority of the metaphors involved cross-sensory mappings (e.g. 'The singer's voice was warm and soft, like pushing around fine grey sand') but some involved more general references to the physical impact of the sensory experience being described (e.g. 'Her voice is very heavy and thick and makes me feel like I'm sinking down slowly under dark water') and others involved references to more abstract concepts (e.g. 'those cookies tasted of regret and rotting flesh'). In nearly all cases, the relationship between the two experiences was found to be motivated by an attested primary metaphorical mapping (e.g. darkness and light; height and depth; sharpness and bluntness, heaviness and lightness) (Grady, 1997), and/or an attested mapping adjunct (e.g. duration, intensity, valence) (Barnden et al., 2003) and/or visual resemblance (e.g. 'Wild strawberries, they're like little pink fireballs of sour'). The metaphor types that we identified in our data are listed below, with examples:

Pattern and colour (metaphorical responses that combined both patterns and colours)

> *I like hearing cars zoom by because the sound looks like* ***blue slowly fading****, and it's very aesthetically pleasing.*

Containment

> *I don't like any ketchup but Heinz because every other type tastes* ***not contained***

> *I don't like twangy modern country music [. . .] the music seems* ***empty*** *and false. I don't know why.*

Direction and movement

> *I like the way wood grain and granite patterns* ***swim across their surface*** *like drizzled caramel or an oil slick that solidified.*

Heaviness and lightness

> *I find the smell to almost have a* ***weight*** *of its own. It feels* ***heavy*** *in the air.*

Height and depth

> *The textures of the music they create are so often much* ***deeper*** *. . . than most modern music.*

Lightness and darkness

> *I hate hearing pure* ***bright*** *high singing because it sounds like jagged white walls and they become overwhelming and* ***bright****.*

Cleanliness and dirtiness

> *I don't like pine because it is too strong, it feels* ***impure****.*

Sharpness and bluntness

> *Very high-pitched noises . . . terrify me. If any of my skin is left uncovered when I hear these sounds, I NEED them to be covered immediately, or at the least I need to get off of the ground.* ***They feel like thousands of red hot needles stabbing in to every inch of my body over and over*** *. . .*

Texture: smooth and rough, soft and hard

> *His voice feels* ***smooth and slick***
>
> *However, the singer's voice was warm and* ***soft, like pushing around fine grey sand****, and when the harmonies came in during the chorus, it was* ***like the sand was being poured over your hands****.*

Structure and shape and pattern

> *[The music of Bach] . . . reminds me of a large, beautiful cathedral –* ***magnificent in its structure, beautiful in its lines, gorgeous in all the small, intimate details.***

Warmth and coldness

> *The best way for me to explain it is that these flavors are all* ***warm*** *to me, even though they're very different . . . The tastes I would group together as* ***warm*** *are chocolate, cinnamon, nutmeg, and banana.*
>
> *It is the color of potential, and it feels like a* ***cold breeze*** *blowing across my back, but under my skin.*

Order and chaos

> *The normal bright colors caused by each horn are replaced by a* ***big mess*** *of dull color and shape.*

The metaphors were also coded according to whether they were creative. Our criteria for identifying creativity involved a combination of approaches employed by Lakoff and Turner (2009), Pérez-Sobrino et al. (2022), Musolff (2016) and Fuoli et al. (2021). Metaphors were coded as creative if they met one or more of the following criteria:

a) They involved comparisons that brought together disparate entities that are not normally compared (e.g. 'I like the way wood grain and granite patterns swim across their surface like drizzled caramel or an oil slick that solidified'; patterns are not conventionally described in terms of food or oil slicks). These are akin to what Pérez-Sobrino et al. (2022) describe as 'one-off source domains'.
b) They involved creative realisations of wide-scope mappings (see Pérez-Sobrino et al., 2022), akin to what Lakoff and Turner (2009) would describe as 'extension' or 'elaboration' of an existing conceptual metaphor. These sometimes involved extended metaphorical mappings; for example, the response '[The music of Bach] reminds me of a large, beautiful cathedral – magnificent in its structure, beautiful in its lines, gorgeous in all the small, intimate details' (see Section 1) sets up a mapping between Bach's music and a cathedral, then provides further explanation of how different elements of the 'cathedral' map on to the music.
c) They involved the creation of dynamic scenarios (Musolff, 2016) in which changes in the sensory experience are explained through changes in the scenario (e.g. 'The guitar gives the sound some depth . . . hiding something powerful under the surface that comes out whenever the song goes from quiet to loud').
d) They involved the juxtaposition of two or more different metaphorical ideas, akin to what Lakoff and Turner (2009) would describe as 'combination'. For example, the response 'His voice melts my mind and makes me warm. His voice looks like deep dark colors and it is my favorite sound' involves connections being made between the voice and (a) heat and (b) colour. In cases such as this, the two metaphors were counted separately, but the fact that they had been juxtaposed in this way meant that we coded them as 'creative', following Lakoff and Turner.
e) They involved form-based creativity (see Fuoli et al., 2021), involving for example, the use of alliteration or assonance (see Carter, 2015).

By coding the responses of the synaesthetes and the non-synaesthetes using these categories, we were able to establish the extent to which the responses produced by synaesthetes and non-synaesthetes differed from one another in terms of the senses employed, the types of response provided, and the metaphorical mappings that were drawn upon. Because we had coded the responses according to the valence and sense of the stimuli, we were also able to assess the extent to which the relationships were affected by the valence of the question and the senses involved. We present the findings from this part of our study in Section 3.

3 '. . . and Rotting Flesh': How Do Synaesthetes and Non-synaesthetes Evaluate Sensory Experiences? What We Found . . .

3.1 Introduction

As we saw in Section 1, the overarching aim of the study described in this book is to explore the nature of 'creativity', specifically metaphorical creativity, by examining it through the lens of synaesthesia. We seek to identify factors of synaesthetes' responses that could be considered 'creative' or may even motivate creativity, and to compare their responses to those produced by non-synaesthetes.

In Section 2, we described the methodology employed in the first part of our study. We found that synaesthetes produced much longer responses than non-synaesthetes and suggested that this difference may reflect the fact that synaesthetes' sensory experiences are in some way 'richer' than those of their non-synaesthete counterparts as not only do they experience the stimulus through the primary sense, they also have access to the associations this stimulus triggers.

In this section, we go into more detail on the nature of responses given by synaesthetes and non-synaesthetes when describing positive and negative sensory experiences. We start by providing a flavour of the ways in which synaesthetes and non-synaesthetes differ in terms of the use they make of the senses in their responses. We then move on to our exploration of the differences between the two groups in terms of use that they made of the response types that were described in Section 2. We focus in particular on the metaphorical themes that they draw on.

Tables showing data on the responses produced for each sense, split by valency, can be found in the additional resources. **Tables A4** and **A5** show the sense responses produced by synaesthetes and non-synaesthetes respectively. **Tables A6** and **A7** show the response types produced by synaesthetes and non-synaesthetes respectively. **Tables A8** and **A9** show the metaphor themes produced by synaesthetes and non-synaesthetes respectively. **Tables A10** and **A11** show the correlations between the response types produced by synaesthetes and non-synaesthetes respectively.

3.2 How Do the Synaesthetes and the Non-synaesthetes Compare with One Another in Terms of the Senses That They Employ in Their Responses?

Given that a key characteristic of synaesthesia is a tendency to describe one sensory experience in terms of another, one would expect to find more references to the senses overall, and more cross-sensory mappings in the descriptions provided by the synaesthetes than in those provided by the non-synaesthetes. We therefore looked at the range of sense types involved in the descriptions provided by each group and investigated the extent to which they cross sensory boundaries when describing their experiences. We also investigated whether the senses used by the synaesthetes in their descriptions resembled those used by the non-synaesthetes, and the extent to which their response patterns resembled those that have been reported in the literature on cross-sensory associations.

Our results are shown in **Tables A4 and A5** in the additional resources, and are summarised in Tables 1 and 2.

As expected, synaesthetes drew on the senses a lot more than the non-synaesthetes, (210 times versus 61), and they made use of a wider range of senses, often when describing a single sensory experience. In the following example, a synaesthete draws on taste, smell, sound, sight and touch to describe the experience of eating bananas and honey:

> *On their own, bananas and honey are already miraculous ... But, combined? ... I take a bite, and ...* ***It smells like rain. It sounds like a deep pink/ blue noise. It looks like a beautiful, opalescent fractal. It feels like velvet all over my body.***

Meanwhile, the non-synaesthetes did produce cross-sensory mappings, but these were largely limited to the sense of touch, which coheres with corpus-based studies showing that touch words are inherently more 'multisensory' than words relating to the other senses (Strik Lievers, 2015).

Some researchers investigating the use of cross-sensory associations in the general population have suggested that there is a 'hierarchy' of the senses, with some senses being more likely than others to be used as the source of cross-sensory associations. The earliest proponents of this idea were Ullmann (1967) and Williams (1976), who proposed that 'touch' is the sense that is most likely to be used to talk about other sensory experiences, followed by taste and then smell, with sight and sound being most likely to be the *target* of the description. Although there is some empirical support for this hierarchy (Day, 1996; Shen, 1997; Shen & Cohen, 1998; Strik Lievers, 2015; Wise, 2003), it has been critiqued in a recent corpus-based study by Winter (2019), who questions the idea of a *monolithic*

Table 1 Use of the senses in responses by synaesthetes

Synaesthetes			
Sense	Number of uses in responses	What sensory experiences did participants use this sense to describe? (No. of uses)	When participants wrote about this sensory experience, what senses did they use to describe it? (No. of uses)
Touch	104	Taste (30), sound (24), sight (23), touch (18), smell (9)	Touch (18), sight (7), sound (3), taste (1)
Sight	75	Sound (30), smell (16), taste (12), sight (10), touch (7)	Touch (23), sight (10), sound (2), taste (1), smell (1)
Taste	20	Taste (9), smell (8), sight (1), sound (1), touch (1)	Touch (30), sight (12), taste (9), smell (2), sound (2)
Sound	8	Touch (3), taste (2), sight (2), smell (1)	Sight (30), touch (24), taste (1)
Smell	3	Taste (2), sight (1)	Sight (16), touch (9), taste (8), sound (1)
Total use of senses in responses: **210**			

Table 2 Use of the senses in responses by non-synaesthetes

Non-synaesthetes			
Sense drawn upon in responses (no. of uses):	Number of uses in responses	What sensory experiences did participants use this sense to describe? (No. of uses)	When participants wrote about this sensory experience, what senses did they use to describe it? (No. of uses)
Touch	39	Touch (14), taste (12), smell (6), sound (4), sight (3)	Touch (14)
Taste	21	Taste (20), smell (1)	Taste (20), touch (12)
Sight	1	Sound (1)	Touch (3)
Sound	0	n/a	Touch (4), sight (1)
Smell	0	n/a	Touch (6), taste (1)
Total use of senses in responses: **61**			

hierarchy and argues for a more nuanced and guarded approach. Interestingly, however, the non-synaesthetes' responses in our study bore a much closer resemblance to Williams' (1976) hierarchy than the synaesthetes' responses.

To sum up, synaesthetes and non-synaesthetes differed considerably in their use of sensory responses. Stimulus-coherent responses were rare in both groups, indicating that cross-sensory mappings are not restricted to synaesthetes. However, synaesthetes drew on a much wider range of senses in their responses than non-synaesthetes. They were also less likely than the non-synaesthetes to adhere to any kind of hierarchy in their cross-sensory mappings.

We also observed differences in the behaviour of the synaesthetes and non-synaesthetes in terms of the valence of sensory experiences which attracted sense-based responses. These differences are shown in Table 3.

Synaesthetes were more likely to draw on the senses when talking about positive items than when talking about negative items, whereas this tendency was reversed for the non-synaesthetes. A chi-square test comparing both groups' use of senses in their responses to both positive and negative stimuli showed this difference to be statistically significant $\chi^2 (1, N = 40) = 4.86, p = .03$. These findings suggest that for the synaesthetes, sensory responses form part of their usual way of conceptualising and processing experiences, both positive or negative, whereas for non-synaesthetes sensory responses are more likely to be used for negative experiences. However, it should be noted that this propensity seems largely driven by the 'taste' sense, which was used for negative responses almost twice as much as for positive responses.

We have seen in this section that when describing sensory experiences, synaesthetes differed considerably from non-synaesthetes in terms of the frequency with which they made cross-sensory associations, the senses that they drew on and the range of senses employed. They had much more to say about the experiences, especially the positive ones; they were more likely to make

Table 3 Total uses of sense-based responses, split by population and valence

	SYNAESTHETES			NON-SYNAESTHETES		
Response sense	**Positive**	**Negative**	**Total**	**Positive**	**Negative**	**Total**
Sight	49	26	75	1	0	1
Smell	1	2	3	0	0	0
Sound	3	5	8	0	0	0
Taste	15	5	20	8	13	21
Touch	55	49	104	17	22	39
Total	**123**	**87**	**210**	**26**	**35**	**61**

cross-sensory associations; they employed a wider range of senses; and their responses did not follow the hierarchy of the senses model as closely as the non-synaesthetes. The synaesthetes' propensity to make connections between a wider range of senses than non-synaesthetes could be said to constitute a form of associative fluency which, as we saw in Section 1, is involved in creative production. According to Fainsilber and Ortony's (1987) 'inexpressibility hypothesis', the need to describe an experience that is not shared tends to attract more metaphor as a means to make one's message understood, and it is reasonable to assume that these metaphors may also be more 'creative' due to a lack of conventional mappings to draw upon. On the other hand, the senses that the non-synaesthetes draw on are more likely to follow conventional patterns, and to cohere with research into the hierarchy of the senses. The fact that these are conventional means that they do not require further elaboration or explanation, and may therefore be less likely to provoke creative output. These sensory directions motivate a large number of conventional metaphors (e.g. *smooth jazz*). In the next section, we dig more deeply into the types of responses provided, with a view to exploring the extent to which the synaesthetes do indeed produce more 'creative' responses to express their experiences as expected.

3.3 How Do the Synaesthetes and the Non-synaesthetes Compare with One Another in Terms of Their Response Types?

In this section, we turn to one of the core questions underpinning our study: what do synaesthetes do when asked to describe positive and negative sensory experiences that non-synaesthetes do not do, and what might this tell us about the factors that trigger the production of creative metaphor? In order to answer this question, we look at the types of response that were triggered by the different sensory experience prompts, explore differences according to the valence of the stimuli and investigate the ways in which the synaesthetes differed from the non-synaesthetes in terms of their response types. Here we compare synaesthetes with non-synaesthetes in terms of their tendency to produce the different response types introduced in Section 2, and look at their answers in detail to help understand how the more general behaviour of the synaesthetes might help explain their greater use of creative metaphor. The numbers of each type of response produced by each of the two groups are shown in **Tables A6 and A7** in the additional resources, and summarised in Table 4.

We can see from Table 4 that the synaesthetes produced far more tokens of these response types overall (556) than the non-synaesthetes (318). This is to be

Table 4 Response types split by population and valence

	Synaesthetes			Non-Synaesthetes		
	Positive	**Negative**	**Total**	**Positive**	**Negative**	**Total**
Emotional effects[b]	78	61	139	52	38	90
Cognitive effects[a]	16	12	28	2	4	6
Physical effects[b]	32	75	107	17	40	57
Personification[b]	16	13	29	4	5	9
Empathy	1	5	6	0	1	1
Value judgements	3	10	13	2	5	7
'Hyperbole'[b]	1	10	11	0	0	0
Literal explanations and associations[a]	35	19	54	59	57	116
Metaphor[a]	74	48	122	9	6	15
Total	178	192	370	93	118	211

([a]significant difference found using a two-tailed test; [b]significant difference found using a one-tailed test)

expected, given the fact that the synaesthetes produced longer texts overall than the non-synaesthetes. We can also see that synaesthetes were more likely than non-synaesthetes to produce responses involving metaphor, cognitive effects, emotional effects, empathy, personification, value judgements, physical effects and hyperbole. In contrast, non-synaesthetes were more likely than synaesthetes to produce responses involving literal explanations and associations. In order to establish whether any of these responses were significantly more likely to be favoured by one of the groups, we conducted Mann-Whitney *U* Tests.[6] Independent variables were the two groups, and dependent variables were the response types. The results are shown in Table 5.

The response types provided by the two groups did not differ significantly in terms of the valence of the sensory experiences. Both groups demonstrated similar patterns of response types in response to negative and positive sensory experiences, and where differences are observed (e.g. in the 'personification' response type, where synaesthetes seem to produce personification more in response to positive sensory experiences whereas non-synaesthetes produce it more in response to negative sensory experiences), the numbers are too small to be able to generalise. However, one point of interest here is that these findings differ from our findings regarding the *senses* that participants drew on in their responses, where we saw a marked difference in the use of senses across the two groups. As we saw above, synaesthetes produced noticeably more examples of sensory responses when describing positive sensory experiences whereas for the non-synaesthetes, the difference was less marked. For response type, however, both groups produced more responses for negative sensory experiences than for positive sensory experiences. It seems that, when examined through the lens of response type rather than response sense, the importance of valence is less marked. However, it is interesting to note how the two groups differ in their behaviour. While both groups produced more response types for negative sensory experiences, the trend towards negativity was slightly stronger in the non-synaesthetes than for the synaesthetes. Again, this suggests that the negativity bias discussed in Section 1 may be slightly weaker in synaesthetes than in non-synaesthetes.

We were also interested to see whether there were any significant relationships between the different response types within each of the two groups. The existence of such relationships might suggest that these processes are somehow

[6] The Mann-Whitney *U* test is the non-parametric equivalent of the independent samples *t*-test. It allows the researcher to investigate whether the distributions of the responses in the two samples are significantly different from one another. The test involves pooling the observations from the two samples into one combined sample, keeping track of which sample each observation comes from, and then ranking lowest to highest from 1 to $n1+n2$, respectively.

Table 5 Response types that were more likely to be favoured by synaesthetes and non-synaesthetes

Response types that were significantly more likely to be provided by synaesthetes	Response types that were more frequent in the synaesthetes' data but where the difference was not statistically significant	Response types that were significantly more likely to be provided by non-synaesthetes
Metaphor	Empathy	Literal responses
(two-tailed $U = 32$, $n1 = n2 = 20$, $P < .05$)	(two-tailed $U =$ ns)	(two-tailed $U = 45.5$, $n1 = n2 = 20$, $P < .05$)
Emotional effects	(one-tailed $U =$ ns)	
(two-tailed $U =$ ns)	Value judgements	
(one-tailed $U = 129.5$, $n1 = n2 = 20$, $P < .05$)	(two-tailed $U =$ ns)	
Cognitive effects	(one-tailed $U =$ ns)	
(two-tailed $U = 118$, $n1 = n2 = 20$, $P < .05$)		
Physical effects		
(two-tailed $U =$ ns)		
(one-tailed $U = 132.5$, $n1 = n2 = 20$, $P < .05$)		
Personification		
(two-tailed $U =$ ns)		
(one-tailed $U = 130$, $n1 = n2 = 20$, $P < .05$)		
'Hyperbole'		
(two-tailed $U =$ ns)		
(one-tailed $U = 130$, $n1 = n2 = 20$, $P < .05$)		

linked. We therefore ran a series of Spearman correlation tests across all major response types for each group of participants separately.[7] We hypothesised that there would be more inter-relationships in the responses produced by the synaesthetes, given their heightened levels of neural connectivity. The findings from these analyses are shown in **Tables A10** and **A11** in the additional resources. As expected, there were far more significant correlations between the variables in the synaesthetes' data than in the non-synaesthetes data. For the synaesthetes, there were significant positive correlations between: cognitive effects and metaphor ($\rho = .24$); cognitive effects and emotional effects ($\rho = .29$); emotional effects and physical effects ($\rho = .28$); emotional effects and empathy ($\rho = .17$); emotional effects and metaphor ($\rho = .19$); empathy and physical response ($\rho = .26$); 'hyperbole' and personification ($\rho = .15$); value judgements and metaphor ($\rho = .17$); metaphor and personification ($\rho = .18$). There was also a significant negative correlation between literal explanations and physical effects ($\rho = -.16$). For the non-synaesthetes, however, there were only two significant positive correlations. These were between cognitive effects and physical effects ($\rho = .17$), and cognitive effects and personification ($\rho = .25$). There were also three significant negative correlations, where literal explanations were shown to negatively correlate with cognitive effects ($\rho = -.14$), emotional effects ($\rho = -.15$), and physical effects ($\rho = -.15$). This finding may suggest that when describing emotional, physical or cognitive effects, literal language is inadequate, which provides further support to the growing body of evidence that metaphor is a crucial communicative tool when describing personal, embodied emotional experiences (see Colston & Gibbs, 2021; Littlemore & Turner, 2019; Semino, 2011).

We can see from these findings that the responses of the synaesthetes were characterised by higher levels of metaphor and emotional, cognitive and physical effects, and, to a lesser extent, empathy, personification, value judgements and hyperbole than those of the non-synaesthetes, and the response types were more interrelated in the synaesthetes. It is particularly interesting to note that in the synaesthetes, three of the response types (cognitive effects, emotional effects and value judgements) correlate with metaphor, suggesting that the desire to communicate experiences such as these may trigger the production of metaphor. Thus, a picture is beginning to emerge of the ways in which synaesthetes respond when asked to evaluate sensory experiences, including a list of features that distinguishes their responses from those provided by non-synaesthetes.

[7] The Spearman correlation test is a non-parametric alternative to the Pearson correlation test. It measures the extent of association between two variables. Each observation reflects the number of responses from a particular category of response type for each individual.

In order to provide a fuller picture of the differences between the two groups in terms of the ways in which they responded to the prompts, it is useful to investigate their responses in a more qualitative manner. We consider here (a) the responses that were significantly likely to be favoured by the synaesthetes, (b) responses that were more frequent in the synaesthetes' data but where the difference was not statistically significant and (c) the responses that were significantly more likely to be favoured by the non-synaesthetes. We now examine each of these response types in detail and explore specific examples. By bringing together these quantitative and qualitative findings, we hope to provide a picture of how the thinking patterns of synaesthetes differ from those of non-synaesthetes in terms of the factors that accompany the production of (creative) metaphor.

3.3.1 Response Types That Were Significantly More Likely to Be Favoured by Synaesthetes

As we saw above, the response types that were significantly more likely to be favoured by the synaesthetes than by the non-synaesthetes were metaphor, cognitive effects, emotional effects, physical effects, personification and 'hyperbole'. Here we look at each of these response types in turn and identify possible reasons for the differences which may help to explain the facility that synaesthetes appear to have regarding the production of metaphor.

3.3.2 Metaphor

We begin our discussion by focusing on the response type that is of central interest to our study: metaphor. A key finding in this study is that synaesthetes produced significantly more metaphor than non-synaesthetes. As we saw in Section 2, we coded responses for metaphor in cases where a participant produced a response that involved describing one experience in terms of another. In all cases, the relationship between the two experiences was motivated by an attested primary metaphorical mapping (pattern and colour; direction and movement; height and depth; heaviness and lightness; lightness and darkness; cleanliness and dirtiness; sharpness and bluntness; texture; structure, shape and pattern; warmth and coldness; order and chaos) and/or an attested mapping adjunct (e.g. duration, intensity, valence, orderliness) (see Barnden et al., 2003). For example, the response 'I love music with a good base (sic.) because base is a deep purple and adds a lot of depth to music for me' transfers an idea of 'intensity' from the auditory experience to the visual experience whilst drawing on a conventional mapping involving depth. In some rarer cases, the metaphors were based on visual resemblance.

We found that the synaesthetes produced significantly more metaphors than the non-synaesthetes, and they also produced significantly more metaphors drawing on pattern and colour, sharpness and bluntness, and texture. The numbers of metaphors of each type (e.g. metaphor involving patterns and colour, direction and movement) that were produced by synaesthetes and non-synaesthetes are shown in Tables A8 and A9 in the additional resources, and summarised in Table 6.

Of the 159 metaphors in the dataset, the vast majority (153) were used creatively. Of the six conventional uses, three were produced by synaesthetes and three by non-synaesthetes. As we saw in Section 2, creative uses of metaphor were more likely to involve playful uses of extending metaphorical ideas than brand new mappings. These included, for example, juxtaposing two entities that are not normally related to one another, introducing more detail into a conventional mapping, or extending it in a novel way; combining two or more conventional metaphors in a novel way; and introducing dramatic contrast. The creative uses of metaphor all involved cross-sensory mappings. Here we

Table 6 Metaphorical mappings drawn upon by synaesthetes and non-synaesthetes

	Synaesthetes	**Non-synaesthetes**
Pattern and colour (two-tailed $U = 80$, $n1 = n2 = 20$, $P < .05$)	55	0
Containment	8	0
Direction and movement	6	4
Heaviness and lightness	2	1
Height and depth	4	0
Lightness and darkness	6	0
Cleanliness and dirtiness	4	1
Sharpness and bluntness (one-tailed $U = 134$, $n1 = n2 = 20$, $P < .05$)	13	4
Texture (two-tailed $U = 100$ $n1 = n2 = 20$, $P < .05$)	18	0
Structure, shape and pattern	8	1
Warmth and coldness	15	3
Order and chaos	5	1
Total	**144**	**15**

illustrate the different kinds of creativity through the use of examples of the kinds of metaphors that were produced. All of these metaphors were produced by synaesthetes (who produced by far the most instances of metaphor).

As a first example, let us consider this response:

> *The ocean smells very yellow. Courage and buoyancy. I love it.*

Here, the respondent extends the conventional association between the colour yellow and positive experiences (Kaya & Epps, 2004) to talk about courage and buoyancy, whilst mapping an olfactory experience onto a visual one. The idea of buoyancy combines the two meanings of the word: 'keeping afloat' and 'feeling happy', which is appropriate given the nature of the subject matter.

In a second example, a respondent says the following of 'cellos:

> *They remind me of childhood when I would slide across ice on my tummy. So smooth, with resistance.*

Here, the respondent extends the conventional metaphor in which music sounds 'smooth' by evoking a specific, personal memory of physical smoothness, thus expressing an auditory experience through reference to a tactile experience which, whilst novel, can also be traced back to a conventional mapping.

This kind of novel extension of a conventional mapping can also be found in the following example:

> *The singer's voice was warm and soft, like pushing around fine grey sand.*

Here the respondent describes an auditory experience in terms of a tactile experience, and extends the conventional idea of a voice sounding 'warm and soft' into a single experience that combines both of these features, but which has additional features, for example the graininess of the sand, or the way in which the sand moves. These features are made available by our ability to picture or even simulate this physical experience, and thus lend an element of creative richness to the description. These last two examples show how, in many cases, the synaesthetes drew on embodied experiences and incorporated them into their metaphorical descriptions in order to convey the richness of their sensory experiences.

Some creative uses of metaphor involved rich descriptions of cross-sensory experiences that involved making comparisons between entities that are not normally related. We can see this in the following example, which was also discussed in Section 1:

> *[The music of Bach] . . . reminds me of a large, beautiful cathedral – magnificent in its structure, beautiful in its lines, gorgeous in all the small, intimate details.*

Here, an auditory experience (listening to music) is described in terms of a visual experience (looking at a cathedral), and the elaborateness of the music is expressed through the elaborateness of the cathedral and the attention to detail that is shown in its architecture. This metaphor draws on a conventional ontological metaphor in which physical structure represents abstract (in this case musical) structure. However, it then develops the metaphor in terms of specificity (a cathedral as opposed to a more general structure or building), the level of detail provided, and extremeness (it is almost hyperbolic in its enthusiasm for the music of Bach).

Another example where a conventional metaphorical mapping was developed into a rich scenario that was described in a detailed way is the following:

> *An example of a voice I don't want to hear (not that it's not a nice voice, it's just uncomfortable to listen to), is the song 'Royals' by Lorde.* ***Her voice is very heavy and thick and makes me feel like I'm sinking down slowly under dark water.***

Here, the conventional metaphorical idea that unpleasantness is 'heavy' is developed into the idea that this particular unpleasant experience is so heavy that it is dragging the respondent down into dark water. The references to 'sinking down' and 'dark' water evoke two further conventional metaphors, in which negative experiences are described as being 'dark' or involving 'downwards' movement (Winter, 2014).

In some cases, the creativity involved drawing attention to contrasting metaphorical experiences, which in themselves constituted developments of conventional metaphorical associations. We can see this in the following example:

> *Songs played in the minor key, and/or soft, lilting music. These are blue and brown songs to me, and I find peace in them. I also like energetic music with a good, driving rhythm because the redness of the songs invigorate me.*

Here, the respondent extends conventional associations that the colours red and blue have with excitement and calmness respectively (Clarke & Costall, 2008), incorporates them into cross-sensory mappings where auditory experiences are described in terms of visual experiences and then contrasts the two experiences with one another by exploiting the natural opposition between the colours red and blue.

Other examples involved the creative use of attested mapping adjuncts (Barnden et al., 2003). In the following example, the respondent maps the idea of a 'lack of orderliness' from the auditory realm onto the visual realm by associating individual sounds with individual colours. When the different (and in their mind incompatible) sounds of car horns are all heard at once, their corresponding colours all merge into a single dull colour which has no definable shape:

> *I hate hearing car horns beep without harmony because the normal bright colors caused by each horn are replaced by a big mess of dull color and shape.*

Similarly, in this next example there is a metaphorical mapping from the disordered nature of the patterns to the discordant nature of the piano playing. The participant thus draws on the domain of music in order to map the jarring nature of a visual experience onto an auditory sensory experience:

> *Peacocks. I hate the patterning.* ***It's like somebody playing the piano out of tune.*** *It's awful.*

Some of the metaphors produced by the synaesthetes expressed extreme responses to the sensory experiences, as we can see in the following example:

> *Very high-pitched noises . . . terrify me. If any of my skin is left uncovered when I hear these sounds, I NEED them to be covered immediately, or at the least I need to get off of the ground. They feel like thousands of red hot needles stabbing into every inch of my body over and over.*

In this example, the respondent employs a conventional metaphor (the idea that a high-pitched sound can be 'piercing') and takes it to what seem like 'hyperbolic' proportions by saying that they feel like 'red hot needles stabbing into every inch' of their body. This example was also coded as 'hyperbole' (see below). The example is illustrative of an interesting feature of our study. For many synaesthetes, the descriptions that they were providing were in some ways 'literally' true but to the reader, they look like creative uses of metaphor. This is indicative of a notion that runs through metaphor studies: the idea that metaphoricity is often in the eye of the beholder and that what may appear metaphorical to the analyst may not in fact have been seen as a metaphor by the person who produced it (Steen, 2008). However, as we saw in Section 1, intentionality is not a necessary prerequisite of creativity, and this is also true of (creative) metaphor (Gibbs, 2015). It is these unintentional, automatic metaphorical associations that form the basis of the kind of creativity that is of interest to us.

There was also some evidence of the creative use of mixed metaphors where a concrete target domain was described in terms of both an emotion and a concrete source domain:

> *Those cookies tasted of* ***regret and rotting flesh****.*

In this example, the respondent combines reference to an abstract emotion (regret) and a physical entity (rotting flesh). Through the reference to rotting flesh, he/she is able to convey taste, smell and possibly texture. The fact that there is a degree of alliteration across the two terms adds to the creativity of this example.

Another example of mixed metaphor is the following:

> *The guitar gives the sound some depth, like a dark background hiding something powerful under the surface that comes out whenever the song goes from quiet to loud.*

Here the participant combines ideas of light and dark with ideas of containment and also a degree of animacy, in order to create a rich scenario which describes the sound of the guitar. Another example of a mixed metaphor is the following:

> *I hate hearing pure bright high singing because it sounds like jagged white walls and they become overwhelming and bright.*

Here, the participant makes metaphorical reference to patterns and colour, lightness and darkness, and sharpness versus bluntness.

Although the synaesthetes produced significantly more of these creative cross-sensory metaphors than the non-synaesthetes, those metaphors that were produced by the non-synaesthetes had similar characteristics. Here are examples of some of the metaphors that were produced by non-synaesthetes:

> *I like to hear the dawn chorus.* ***It is like a warm bath*** *– feels soothing.*
>
> *I love the smell of freshly baked goodies . . . when re-entering the house or room* ***it hugs you like a warm blanket****.*
>
> *I do not like to smell fish that has gone rotten.* ***It is like the sharp rocks – feels jagged and repelling****. I do not like it because of its sharpness and makes me feel a little ill.*

Like the examples produced by the synaesthetes, these examples also involve new combinations that involve cross-sensory mappings, and that draw on existing conventional metaphorical associations. The first two examples draw on the relationship between pleasantness and warmth and the third example extends the idea that smells (like tastes) can be 'sharp'.

What we see in all of these examples are descriptions of novel embodied metaphorical experiences. The linguistic descriptions of these experiences contain metaphors that are novel yet principled and contextually meaningful. They therefore display the hallmarks of creativity in that they combine *novelty* with *appropriacy* (Carter, 2015). Some of the types of creativity in our data resembled those found in earlier work, where we analysed creative uses of metaphor in a film review database (Fuoli et al., 2021). However, some of the types of creativity that were found in our earlier work, such as those involving recontextualisation and appropriation, were not found in this study, probably because the responses in this study were more spontaneous, and less 'crafted' or 'performative' as they were not being written for a public audience. This reflects the genre-/register-based nature of variation in creative metaphor use (see Deignan et al., 2013).

The fact that these experiences are reported more frequently by the synaesthetes is likely to have derived from their heightened propensity to form cross-sensory associations when recalling positive or negative sensory experiences. The two groups performed similarly in terms of the senses that were most likely to provoke the use of these metaphors. Of all the senses studied we found that sound was most likely to trigger the use of these creative cross-sensory metaphors in both synaesthetes and non-synaesthetes. This finding is in line with previous work in the area; in their wide-ranging study of the ways in which speakers of twenty-one languages from across the world describe sensory experiences, Majid et al. (2018) found that sound was more likely to attract metaphorical descriptions than the other modalities.

Interestingly, synaesthetes were more likely than non-synaesthetes to produce these creative cross-sensory metaphors when discussing positive sensory experiences than when discussing negative ones. This suggests that the production of creative metaphor in synaesthetes does not result from memories of negative experiences, presumably because the positive experiences were just as rich and memorable (Meier & Rothen, 2013). Synaesthetes may differ from non-synaesthetes in this respect. For the synaesthetes, the production of creative cross-sensory metaphor was found to correlate with descriptions of cognitive, emotional and physical effects, which suggests that a high level of engagement with the stimulus drives the production of metaphor by synaesthetes. We now look at these categories in more depth.

3.3.3 Cognitive Effects

As we saw in Section 2, the 'cognitive effects' category was used for examples where participants were describing an object or experience which had an effect on the way they thought. They might report, for example that 'my thoughts become odd'. The synaesthetes were significantly more likely than the non-synaesthetes to produce these kinds of responses when discussing the sensory experiences. This suggests that synaesthetes have a stronger psychological response to sensory experiences. Furthermore, references to cognitive effects correlated with the production of metaphor and references to emotional effects.

The synaesthetes were more likely to report 'cognitive effects' when talking about positive sensory experiences, while the non-synaesthetes were more likely to do so when talking about negative sensory experiences. This reflects the general tendency for synaesthetes to be forthcoming in their responses to positive sensory experiences in comparison to non-synaesthetes. One reason why cognitive effects in particular tended to be associated with more positive sensory experiences in the synaesthetes may reflect the fact that sensory experiences tend to have a stronger psychological impact on them. For the synaesthetes, a pleasurable sensory experience could quite literally alter their state of mind in dramatic ways which could only be expressed through metaphor:

> *It feels as though I'm drifting away from reality when I hear violins. It's a remarkable experience, and words could never properly capture what it's like.*

For both synaesthetes and non-synaesthetes, negative sensory experiences triggered these kinds of response, but in synaesthetes the responses tended to be more elaborate. For example, here are two responses produced by synaesthetes:

> *Really, really loud rock music.* ***It's like it sucks the brains out of my head*** *... Physical pain plus* ***obliteration of any sort of thinking or feeling*** *is why I hate it.*
>
> *It is as though the noise* ***shuts my brain down for a moment*** *and* ***I can think of nothing other than escaping the noise*** *as my body reacts without my conscious awareness.*

In contrast to these rich descriptions, when non-synaesthetes produced responses in the 'cognitive effects' category, these were less likely to be developed or richly described, as we see in the following examples:

> *[It]* ***takes over your thoughts***
>
> *They make me feel peaceful and* ***they make my brain quiet.***

3.3.4 Emotional Effects

The third characteristic that distinguished the responses provided by the synaesthetes from those provided by the non-synaesthetes was emotional effects. References to emotional effects featured significantly more frequently in the synaesthetes responses than in the non-synaesthetes' responses. We can see examples in the following:

> *One I listened to the other day, the background music was* ***annoying*** *like a twitch or like trying to zip an old metal zipper that keeps getting caught.*
>
> *Songs played in the minor key, and/or soft, lilting music. These are blue and brown songs to me, and* ***I find peace*** *in them. I also like energetic music with a good, driving rhythm because the redness of the songs* ***invigorate*** *me.*

Both groups were more likely to refer to emotions in response to positive sensory experiences than in response to negative sensory experiences. For example, when asked to describe a sight that they liked, one of the synaesthetes commented:

> *I love to see soft wood. It feels like home and feels* ***happy****.*

And one of the non-synaesthetes commented that:

> *Roses – my favourite flower. The smell just* ***lifts my spirits*** *instantly.*

This runs counter to the general negativity bias that was observed for some of the other response types for both synaesthetes and non-synaesthetes. This suggests that respondents chose to refer to emotions when talking about positive sensory experiences than when talking about negative sensory experiences.

Words relating to the senses of taste and smell have been found to be closely linked to emotions (Winter, 2016), perhaps because of the evocative and nostalgic nature of these senses. However, we found that neither the synaesthetes nor the non-synaesthetes produced the most 'emotional effects' responses to taste and smell sensory experiences. In both populations, the sense most likely to produce 'emotional effects' responses was 'sound'. This may relate to other conditions where experiences of sound trigger particular changes in emotions and thought patterns. Misophonia, for example, 'refers to a strong dislike of certain sounds and an abnormally strong reaction to them, characteristically anger and even rage' (Bruxner, 2015, p. 195), while individuals experiencing ASMR (autonomous sensory meridian response) report feelings of relaxation and wellbeing, as well as pleasurable physical sensations in response to particular auditory triggers (Poerio et al., 2018, p. 1). Previous studies have explored the link between tactile experiences and emotion in synaesthetes (Ramachandran & Brang, 2008), but we are unaware of any studies to date that have identified a specific role for auditory sensory experiences in this respect.

We saw in Section 1 that people tend to use more metaphor, particularly creative metaphor, when describing intense emotional experiences. We also saw that metaphor itself can trigger emotional responses in the brain (Citron & Goldberg, 2014), and that exposure to metaphors that draw on sensory activity can trigger responses in the sensory cortex, particularly when they are creative. Finally, we saw that the neural links between the sensory cortex and the amygdala (which is responsible for processing emotion) are stronger in the synaesthete population than in the non-synaesthete population. This suggests that there is a link between creative metaphor, emotion and sensory activation, and that this link is stronger in synaesthetes than in the general population. The fact that the synaesthetes in our study experienced (a) much stronger emotional responses to sensory experiences, (b) more cross-sensory associations and (c) more (creative cross-sensory) metaphor provides strong evidence to suggest that emotion may play a key role in triggering the use of creative metaphor.

3.3.5 Physical Effects

The synaesthetes were also significantly more likely than the non-synaesthetes to refer to the physical effects of the sensory experience. The 'physical effects' category was used for examples where participants described having a physical response to the object or experience being described. Both the synaesthetes and the non-synaesthetes reported more physical effects when describing negative sensory experiences than when describing positive sensory experiences. Here is an example of one such response:

> *I don't like the colour yellow. It's too startling and* ***hurts my brain****. It's sudden.*

The fact that physical effects were more likely to be associated with negative sensory experiences is interesting as it contrasts with our findings for emotional effects.

For both groups, physical effects were most likely to be reported in response to touch-related sensory experiences and sound-related sensory experiences. In both cases, more than twice as many physical effects were reported in response to negative sensory experiences than positive sensory experiences.

When describing things they did not like to touch, both synaesthetes and non-synaesthetes described physical responses to pain (understandably), but in addition to this, the synaesthetes described negative physical responses to non-pain-related phenomena, such as the following:

> *Many coats and some sweatpants have a lining inside them that's supposedly very soft and very warm,* ***but to me it's just suffocating. It makes me feel that if I pressed my face in it, the texture would clog my respiratory system.***
> *I don't like how being loved feels like. It creeps the hell out of me, the* ***involuntary warmth somewhere deep in my chest area and the way my skin crawls along my neck and shoulders****.*

It is interesting that both synaesthetes and non-synaesthetes gave 'physical effects' responses to sound sensory experiences. For the non-synaesthetes, this may be due to the directionality of conventional synaesthetic language, as many languages draw on touch-related language to describe sound (Strik Lievers, 2015). Phenomena such as misophonia and ASMR, as introduced above, may also suggest a link between sound and physiological responses as individuals experiencing these conditions often report such responses.

3.3.6 Personification

The synaesthetes made use of this response type significantly more than the non-synaesthetes, which is in line with previous findings regarding the tendency of some synaesthetes to personify inanimate objects and graphemes (Amin et al., 2011). Here are some examples of the synaesthetes' responses:

> *Ocean air feels like it's* ***calling, 'let me love you!!!'***
>
> *The bass is my favourite instrument. I love its warmth and the way* ***the sound just holds you in a way****.*
>
> *The waves seem* ***angry*** *and* ***I do not trust them***
>
> *Water which is flavored, but only slightly.* ***What are you? Are you water or are you flavored water? Pick something!***

The responses provided by the synaesthetes that involved personification tended to be more elaborate than those of the non-synaesthetes, as we can see in the following example:

> *I absolutely love the color pink. For me, it is ALWAYS associated with a very gentle woman, aged around, perhaps, 25–35. I can feel her wrap her arms around my neck from behind, and she has the most beautiful and gentle smile on her face. She wears a plain white sundress with a straw sunhat. She (pink) makes me feel unbelievably safe, as though nothing could ever possibly go wrong.*

Contrast this with a typical non-synaesthete's response in this category, where the personification is both more conventional and less elaborated:

> *The sea, particularly when it's rough. I like the fact that it's* ***wild and uncontrolled****.*

3.3.7 'Hyperbole'

As we saw in Section 2, the 'hyperbole' category was used in cases where the participant provided an extreme response to the stimulus. The synaesthetes were significantly more likely to produce 'hyperbole', and their use of this response type correlated with personification. Examples of responses in this category are as follows:

> *There are so many smells I don't like. Most of them, really. Above all else, however, is Lemon Pine-Sol. Good lord, are you ready to be grossed out? The moment I smell this stuff, it's over. First, I get angry as HECK just because I have to smell this nasty stuff. But then the worst part hits. Imagine taking a trash bag and filling it with a mass of disgusting filth. Human waste, rotting and decaying food, chemicals, etc., and then fill it with maggots. Now leave that to sit in the sun for about a week to ferment.* ***Empty out all the trash***

> ***inside, turn the bag inside out, and lick the moisture off of the surface. THAT is atrocious taste that it invokes.***
>
> *I'm highly sensitive to long exposure to scents, especially sweet ones. I don't find the smell of bananas repulsive, but if I remain in the same room with one for more than an hour,* ***it drills into my skull and overwhelms me.***
>
> *Scented candles are the worst, and* ***most perfumes when encountered suddenly feel like a physical punch in the lungs.***

Again, the fact that the synaesthetes produced all these responses suggests that they had a higher level of engagement with the sensory experiences. Many of the responses in this category also involved creative cross-sensory metaphor. We can see this in the above examples, where the smell of Lemon Pine-Sol is compared to licking the liquid that seeps out of old rubbish, or where the smell of bananas 'drills into my skull', or the smell of scented candles 'feels like a physical punch in the lungs'. This suggests that the extremity of the experiences may have been a factor in leading the participants to produce creative cross-sensory metaphor.

3.3.8 Response Types That Were More Frequent in the Synaesthetes' Responses but Where the Difference Was Not Statistically Significant

The two response types that were more frequent in the synaesthetes' data but where the difference was not statistically significant were empathy and value judgements.

Empathy

As we saw in Section 2, the 'empathy' category was used for cases where participants expressed a sense of empathy or identification brought on by the object or experience under discussion. It was a somewhat broad category and included both empathy with inanimate objects and more general empathy towards other people. Again, this type of response appeared to be more common in the synaesthetes than in the non-synaesthetes, which is in line with previous research showing that some synaesthetes have been found to exhibit an enhanced propensity for empathy with inanimate objects (Banissy & Ward, 2007) or are more likely to 'feel' the pain of others (Banissy & Ward, 2013). However, perhaps because of the small numbers involved, and perhaps because the category also included more general expressions of empathy with other people (which are not necessarily related to synaesthesia), the difference was not statistically significant. Here is an example of one of the responses produced by a synaesthete that we coded as involving 'empathy':

> *I do not like to see pain or things that are painful or disgusting. When viewing someone get a cut or other bodily damage, it is very difficult not to imagine*

> *the feeling.* ***If someone's having their hand or arm cut, I often shake my arm to get the feeling out****. It is very unpleasant.*

In this example, the respondent relates to and feels sympathy for the people experiencing pain. Only one participant in the study, a synaesthete, reported feeling empathy with *inanimate* objects, as we can see in the following example:

> *The reason this is enjoyable is that it helps to 'empathize' with things that most people probably wouldn't even know you could empathize with; yellow street-lines, beehives, computer monitors, etc . . . (I use empathize in a way similar to, but not exactly like its actual definition. Rather, it is closer to a feeling of 'complete understanding' of that one object).*

Synaesthetes were likely to provide empathetic responses when they were talking about things that they like and do not like to see. They produced none for sound, smell or taste. The only empathy response provided by the non-synaesthetes was also produced in response to sight. These findings resonate with Marks' (2013) ideas relating to physiognomic perception, which were discussed in Section 1. Again, this phenomenon, which has been shown to lead to higher levels of creative metaphor production, is stronger in synaesthetes than in non-synaesthetes.

One possible limitation of our study is that we considered all kinds of empathy together; further research could separate out different kinds of empathy, with different kinds of targets.

Value Judgements

As we saw in Section 2, the 'value judgements' category was used for examples where participants expressed some form of judgement as to how something should or should not be, often with a moral or ethical component. The synaesthetes produced nearly twice as many responses of this type (13) than the non-synaesthetes (7), but the low numbers overall mean that this difference was not statistically significant. The synaesthetes sometimes expressed annoyance when the cross-sensory mappings were somehow 'wrong', suggesting that they had strong feelings about what they 'should' and 'should not' be, as shown in the following two examples:

> *I don't like to smell gasoline because* ***the color of the smell is bright orange but gasoline isn't and that annoys me. Bleach smells light blue but it is actually clear; that annoys me too.***

> *I don't like the smell of burning leaves. It's close to campfire smell (which is pleasant) but it has a weird sour overtone that just makes it smell* ***wrong****.*

This finding chimes with the finding discussed in Section 1 that synaesthetes often react negatively to what they perceive as 'incongruent' associations (Callejas & Lupiáñez, 2013). The responses provided by the non-synaesthetes that fell into this category tended to be less elaborate than those provided by the synaesthetes:

> *Stronger flavours just seem more* ***worthwhile*** *and satisfying.*

Again, these tendencies suggest that the synaesthetes seem to be engaging deeply with the sensory experiences, to the point that they make value judgements.

3.3.9 Response Types That Were Significantly More Likely to Be Favoured by Non-synaesthetes

Only one response type was significantly more likely to be used by non-synaesthetes, and somewhat predictably, this was the literal response type.

Literal Responses

As we saw in Section 2, the 'literal response' category was used for examples where participants were explaining their like or dislike of a particular object or experience by referring in a very literal way to the meaning of the stimulus or drawing on the memories or associations it evokes. Non-synaesthetes made significantly more use than synaesthetes of literal explanations and associations. Here are some examples typical of those produced by the non-synaesthetes:

> *Strong body odour/perspiration.* ***Suggests lack of cleanliness and hygiene.***
>
> *Petunias.* ***It reminds me of a place where we used to go on holiday,*** *where there were lots growing by the main footpath.*
>
> *I love the smell of a dog after the vet* ***because it reminds me of my childhood***
>
> *I do not like the smell of hospitals / disinfectant. The smell is often too strong / overwhelming and* ***I associate it with illness.***

As we can see from these examples, the responses produced by the non-synaesthetes were much more likely to be functional and literal, and were largely lacking in metaphorical creativity. However, despite lacking in metaphorical creativity, some of the responses provided in this category exhibited interesting stylistic features. For example, one participant employed a construction that is usually associated with food to describe themselves as 'over-salted':

> *I do not like the taste of extremely salty things. After a few bites I start feeling uncomfortably over-salted.*

This results in a slightly humorous depersonalisation; the way the participant describes the experience encourages the reader to see it in a new way. This defamiliarisation results in a somewhat humorous effect (see Attardo, 2010; Raskin, 1985). Examples such as these were rare in our study. However, they do suggest that other forms of creativity might be at play which do not involve metaphor, and are deserving of further study.

3.4 Conclusion

The findings from our analysis of the response types that tended to be favoured by the synaesthetes and non-synaesthetes respectively are that, in addition to providing significantly more metaphors, synaesthetes also made significantly more references to cognitive effects, emotions and physical effects, and personification. They also reported more extreme reactions to the experiences, as they were significant more likely to use 'hyperbole'. They also employed somewhat more personification, empathy and references to what 'should or should not be'. Their responses were also more elaborate. In contrast, the responses provided by the non-synaesthetes were more 'straightforward' and literal. The response types were also more correlated in the synaesthetes' responses than in the non-synaesthetes' responses. This suggests that there may be a cluster of behaviours that surround the production of creative cross-sensory metaphor that are particularly prevalent in synaesthetes, and that to some extent these behaviours may *trigger* the use of these metaphors.

Given these findings, we are now in a position to consider the overall differences between synaesthetes' and non-synaesthetes' evaluative descriptions of sensory experiences and what they might tell us about the relationship between emotional, physical and cognitive engagement and creative metaphor. One of the most notable observations from this study relates to the comparative 'richness' of the synaesthetes' responses in comparison with the non-synaesthetes. We already saw in Section 2 that the synaesthetes had more to say than their non-synaesthete counterparts. In this section we have seen that not only do they say more, but they produce a wider variety of responses across the board in terms of response sense, type and metaphorical theme. They also appear to have less of a negativity bias than the non-synaesthetes.

We have also seen in this section that synaesthetes are more likely than non-synaesthetes to produce responses containing metaphor (most of which contained creative, cross-sensory mappings), and they were particularly likely to use metaphor when describing positive sensory experiences. They were also more likely to make reference to emotional, physical and cognitive effects, hyperbole and empathy. Finally, there were more likely to be inter-relationships between the responses types that were used by the synaesthetes. What do these co-occurrences mean and what might they say about the kinds of cross-sensory mappings that synaesthetes form, the factors that motivate them to make these mappings and the extent to which they can be described as 'metaphorical' or 'creative'?

The co-occurrence between metaphor, emotion and cognitive effects in the synaesthetes' data reflects findings in the metaphor literature that internal thought processes and experiences are often talked about using metaphor, as these are often difficult to express in literal terms (Gibbs & Franks, 2002; Littlemore & Turner, 2019; Turner et al., 2020). Synaesthetes are more likely to report strong visceral responses to sensory experiences which can result in physical pain ('it's piercing through my skin') or mental disturbances ('they take over my head and drive me mad'), and they respond on a much more emotional level ('it makes me anxious'). These extreme reactions appear to be linked to their tendency to form cross-sensory associations, many of which have a strong metaphorical feel to them ('I like hearing cars zoom by because the sound looks like blue slowly fading'), and some of which involve personification ('it's indecisive about which pitch it wants to be'). All of these findings point to the embodied nature of creative metaphor generation, which was alluded to in Section 1. They suggest that the richer, and more intense, ways in which synaesthetes engage with sensory experiences may in fact be the trigger for many of the creative metaphors that they produce.

Metaphor has also been shown to be useful as an expressive tool, helping people to conceptualise and communicate experiences that are not widely shared by the rest of the population. With this in mind, it is particularly interesting to note that metaphor was relatively absent in the non-synaesthetes' data. This may be because they are more likely to describe highly conventional emotional responses, which they do not feel the need to draw on metaphor to explain. Also, the experiences that the synaesthetes are describing tend to be more internal as they are often describing the thought processes themselves, whereas the non-synaesthetes tend to draw more on literal associations and memories of external experiences and actions. Compare the response from a synaesthete (a) with a response from a non-synaesthete (b):

> *(a)* ***Really, really loud rock music. It's like it sucks the brains out of my head –so loud it actually hurts. Physical pain plus obliteration of any sort of thinking or feeling is why I hate it.***

> (b) *Petunias.* ***It reminds me of a place where we used to go on holiday,*** *where there were lots growing by the main footpath.*

The synaesthete in (a) draws on metaphor to describe the internal experience itself, whereas the non-synaesthete in (b) remembers a particular event without going into detail on the emotional quality of that memory. This means there is less scope for them to draw on metaphor in their response.

The correlation between cognitive effects and personification in the non-synaesthetes' data may be due to the fact that personification allowed the non-synaesthetes to 'blame' particular sensory experiences for their responses, as in the following example:

> *Loud baseline beat of music –* ***takes over your thoughts*** *and is very unpleasant. Especially if it is so loud you can feel it.*

These findings have interesting implications for the relationship between emotion, creativity and metaphor. It should be remembered that although the metaphorical mappings were creative, they all drew on motivated embodied relationships between physical and emotional experiences, which displayed varying degrees of conventionality. When a synaesthete comments that 'those cookies tasted of regret and rotting flesh' the synaesthete is extending an established embodied relationship between negative emotional experiences and bad flavours (e.g. 'it left a bad taste in my mouth') and juxtaposing this with a more perceptual metaphoric relationship. When a synaesthete comments that 'Her voice is very heavy and thick and makes me feel like I'm sinking down slowly under dark water', he or she is drawing on conventional, embodied metaphorical mappings between the target domain 'sound' and the source domains 'weight', 'darkness' and 'movement', and combining and extending them in a new way.

The reactions reported by the synaesthetes to different sounds were much more physical, emotional and intense than those reported by the non-synaesthetes, as we can see in the following example:

> *[very] high-pitched noises.* ***These terrify me.*** *If any of my skin is left uncovered when I hear these sounds, I NEED them to be covered immediately, or at the least I need to get off of the ground.* ***They feel like thousands of red hot needles stabbing in to every inch of my body over and over, and they look like seeing a fire from INSIDE the fire.***

This may reflect findings from neuro-imaging studies where it has been shown that during sound perception, synaesthetes show significantly more brain activation in the inferior parietal cortex than non-synaesthetes (Neufeld et al., 2012). This area is involved in multimodal integration, the perception of emotions in facial stimuli and, most importantly, the interpretation of sensory information.

To sum up, synaesthetic individuals reported stronger emotional, cognitive and physical effects in response to the sensory experiences and were somewhat more likely to personify the stimuli that triggered those experiences, empathise with, 'judge' them and describe the experiences in extreme terms. These highly 'embodied' responses to the experiences appear to have played a role in their production of creative metaphors, suggesting that embodied metaphor, empathy, emotion, physical experience and creativity are intrinsically linked through a symbiotic relationship, and that this link is particularly prominent in synaesthetes. Synaesthetes have a higher engagement with the sensory experiences, and a desire to communicate this to others. It has been shown in previous research that this kind of communicative need may shape the strategies that people employ when communicating rich sensory experiences (Winter, 2019), leading them to produce metaphor that can be considered to be creative (Caballero, 2009). The responses produced by synaesthetes involved significantly more creative metaphor than those produced by the non-synaesthetes. The fact that synaesthetes' responses were also more likely to involve empathy, references to physical, emotional and cognitive effects, 'hyperbole' and personification suggests that these factors may be implicated in the process of creative metaphor production. Overall, it appears to be the case that synaesthetes experience higher levels of emotional, cognitive and physical engagement with sensory experiences, which can lead them to produce vivid examples of metaphorical language and hyperbole as they explain them.

4 'Yeurgh . . . ': How We Investigated Synaesthetes' and Non-synaesthetes' Responses to Emotion Words and Emotive Expressions, and What We Found

4.1 Introduction

In Section 3, we identified a number of differences in the ways in which synaesthetes and non-synaesthetes described sensory experiences. Our findings suggested that strong emotional engagement with a sensory experience may be a driver of metaphorical creativity. The fact that synaesthetes engaged with sensory experiences on a much more emotional level than the non-synaesthetes appears to have led them to empathise with these stimuli, experience physical and cognitive reactions to them, judge them as 'right' or 'wrong' and talk about their sensory experiences in creative metaphorical ways. If it is the case that heightened emotional experiences seem to lead synaesthetes to produce creative cross-sensory metaphors, is it also the case that they perceive emotion itself in different ways from non-synaesthetes? In order to answer this question, we explored synaesthetes' and non-synaesthetes' responses to emotions in more depth. We were interested in examining whether there are differences in the ways in which synaesthetes understand and respond to emotions. One of the best ways to access people's understandings of a phenomenon is to ask them what they associate it with. By exploring the range of associations that people have with a given phenomenon, we gain in-depth knowledge of the way in which they understand and experience it.

In this section, we introduce a shorter test which participants undertook following the longer writing task. We used a word association task to investigate synaesthetes' and non-synaesthetes' responses to emotion-related words. They were asked to write the first thing that came to mind when they saw the word. As with the writing task discussed in Section 3, we did not specify the required length of the answers. The results provide insights into the different ways in which synaesthetes and non-synaesthetes *understand* and, by extension, *experience* different types of emotions. These insights will allow us to comment further on the relationships between creativity, metaphor and emotion in synaesthetic and non-synaesthetic populations, as first introduced in Section 3.

4.2 Investigating Responses to Emotion Words and Emotive Expressions

4.2.1 Emotion Words: Word Association Task

In the test discussed in this section, we wanted to see whether the synaesthetes' responses to emotion words were in any way reminiscent of their descriptions of sensory experiences. We considered word association an appropriate methodology for this task, as word association tests (hereafter WATs) have been used in a range of disciplines to investigate respondents' cognitive structures, particularly as relating to the learning and understanding of concepts (Simner, 2007) (see e.g. Derman & Eilks, 2016; Lee, 1988 for a discussion of word association methodology used to investigate knowledge of chemistry). Such tests have also been used to explore participants' attitudes and beliefs (see Szabó et al., 2018's use of WATs to explore attitudes towards renewable energy, or Latorres et al., 2016; Rojas-Rivas et al., 2018; Soares et al., 2017 on perceptions of particular foods). We hypothesised that, given the clear differences we identified in the preceding writing task, the WAT would provide further evidence of synaesthetes and non-synaesthetes responding differently to emotion-related stimuli.

While the preceding writing task focused on sensory experiences, here we used words corresponding to the six 'basic' emotions (see Ekman, 1992): happiness, sadness, fear, anger, surprise and disgust. We are aware of some of the controversies surrounding Ekman's categorisation scheme, but our aim was to explore participants' responses to a small number of widely understood emotions, for which we considered Ekman's scheme to be appropriate. Participants were presented with each word in turn and asked to write what came to mind when they read each one. As the test was administered asynchronously online through the Qualtrics system, it was unfortunately not possible to control the amount of time participants actually spent on each word. However, we considered that where participants did provide more in-depth responses than expected, this in itself could provide an interesting indication of how they responded to the prompt, and the level of significance they attributed to it. As we saw in Section 2, synaesthetes produced longer responses to the writing task overall, and we proposed that the less conventional nature of their sensory experiences required greater description and explanation as they were not commonly shared by the rest of the population. On an affective level, too, it became apparent in Section 3 that synaesthetes reported more emotional evaluative descriptions of sensory experiences, and we suggested that the richness and emotional value of their sensory experiences may lead them to spend more time describing them. In the WAT, likewise, a lengthier written response could indicate a similar complexity to their affective responses.

After collecting the participants' responses to the word association prompts, we employed an iterative process to develop a coding scheme which we used to categorise the data. Like the coding scheme developed for the written task described in Section 2, this scheme was developed through thematic analysis over multiple passes of the data. The resulting categories were then arranged into a more manageable coding scheme through merging related areas (for example, the categories 'body parts' and 'facial expressions' were very small, so we assimilated them into the broader 'People, body parts, facial expressions' category).

These categories were not mutually exclusive, and responses could be coded as belonging to more than one of these categories. For example, the response '*family*' would be coded as *abstract concept* and *people, body parts, facial expressions*. Similarly, parts of a response could be split into different categories. For example, the response '*red, blindness, an ox*' in response to 'anger' was coded as 'colour' (red), 'people, body parts, facial expressions' (blindness, due to its link to the eyes) and 'nature and natural phenomena' (an ox). Examples of items in each category are as follows:

Abstract concepts

[Anger] – *Loss of control*
[Happiness] – *Unity*

Actions

[Fear] – *Shaking*
[Surprise] – *Opening my eyes wide*

Colour

[Happiness] – *Yellow*
[Sadness] – *Blue*

Synonyms and related emotions

[Fear] – *Panic*
[Surprise] – *Happiness*

Exclamations and onomatopoeia

[Disgust] – *Yeurgh*
[Surprise] – *OOOOOOH!*

Nature and natural phenomena

[Fear] – *Long skinny trees with long skinny branches hanging down*
[Sadness] – *Death*

People, body parts, facial expressions

[Disgust] – *A person with a frown face looking down their noise at someone.*
[Happiness] – *Smiling*

Physical objects

[Anger] – *Lava lamps*
[Fear] – *Needles*

Physical sensations

[Anger] – *Rising overwhelming feeling in my chest*
[Sadness] – *Pain*

Qualities

[Anger] – *Unnecessary*
[Disgust] – *Vile*

Scenarios

[Anger] – *A cutesy version of an irritated face, red puffs of emotion floating out at regular intervals*

[Sadness] – *A person with a slightly frowning face moving their arms like they're cracking the reins of a horse drawn carriage.*

Synaesthetic associations with letters or sounds of the prompt word

[Fear] – *This word is orange, and feels sharp.*
[Surprise] – *I view a red and blue background with a yellow-outlined oval in the middle.*

After allocating each response to one or more of these categories, we also coded each response for perceived conventionality. The 'conventional' category was used when there was a clear conventional link between the prompt word and the response. In the following examples, *red* is conventionally associated with 'anger' (e.g. Fetterman et al., 2012), and *recoiling* is a natural response to 'fear' as a component of the 'fight or flight' response first identified by Cannon (1929). A response could be coded as 'unconventional' if it met one or more of the following conditions:

a) The response lacked a clear conventional link between the prompt and the response. For example, 'disgust' is not usually associated with *neon pink*, nor 'fear' with *bacon*. However, it must be noted that such responses are likely to have been highly meaningful for the participants themselves, especially in the case of synaesthetic participants, for whom the word 'disgust' may very well be experienced as being 'neon pink' or who may have a disgust response to the colour.
b) A conventional link could reasonably be identified, but the response involved a logical extension from this link. For example, one participant gave the response 'an ox' to the prompt 'anger', possibly due to the aggressive nature of an ox which may have led the participant to associate it with anger.
c) An unusually detailed description of a scenario was provided, which would not be considered a 'conventional' response to an emotional prompt in a word association task. This is demonstrated in the following example, produced by a synaesthete as a response to 'disgust':

> *A food service employee holding her hands to her mouth, eyes alternatingly alarmed and shut as tight as possible as she runs for the bathroom, leaving behind the rotting meat she found behind a piece of kitchen equipment.*

4.3 How Do Synaesthetes and Non-synaesthetes Differ in Their Responses to the Emotion Words WAT?

Here, we explore the responses to the word association task. We begin by observing the general differences between the two groups in terms of their responses to the emotion prompts in the word association task. The first notable difference relates to the overall number of words produced by the two groups, which mirrors the findings observed in our analysis of the sensory stimulus tasks. We observed in Section 2 that the body of writing produced by the synaesthetes in response to the sensory stimulus tasks was over twice as large as the dataset produced by the non-synaesthetes. We posited that synaesthetes' sensory experiences may be somehow more rich or salient to them, although we noted that the self-selecting nature of the participants may also have played a role in this finding, as the synaesthetic participants in our study may have been particularly keen to make their experiences known. However, it is interesting to note that even in a word association task such as this one, the synaesthetes produced more text in response overall, with some synaesthetes providing extended descriptions of scenarios in response to the stimuli. Figures showing how the two groups differed in terms of their response word counts can be found in **Table A12** in the additional resources. In this respect, the behaviours of each group in response to the word association task mirror the findings of the sensory description writing task. This finding may be taken as preliminary evidence that emotional stimuli provoke a similarly rich, vivid response in synaesthetes as do sensory experiences.

As well as producing an observable difference in word count, synaesthetes and non-synaesthetes differed in the extent to which they drew on the range of categories in their responses. The breakdown of response types according to their perceived conventionality is provided in Table 7. As mentioned in Section 4.2, responses could be coded as belonging to more than one category. These figures show that in comparison with the non-synaesthetes, synaesthetes produced more tokens overall (206 vs the non-synaesthetes' 173), and they were significantly more likely to favour unconventional responses over conventional responses than the non-synaesthetes (χ^2 (1, N = 40) = 109.64, p >.00001). This mirrors the finding reported in Section 3 that synaesthetes produced more extensive and detailed descriptions of sensory experiences than non-synaesthetes. Similar patterns are therefore observed in synaesthetes' responses to both sensory and emotional stimuli, which may provide further evidence for the highly embodied, emotionally rich nature of their experiences.

We can see from Table 7 that synaesthetes were more likely than non-synaesthetes to produce responses involving 'actions', 'colour', 'nature and natural phenomena', 'people, body parts and facial expressions', 'physical objects', 'scenarios', and 'synaesthetic associations'. In contrast, non-synaesthetes were more likely than synaesthetes to produce responses involving 'abstract concepts', 'synonyms and related emotions', 'exclamations and onomatopoeia', 'physical sensations' and 'qualities'. In order to establish which of these responses were

Table 7 Response types produced by synaesthetes and non-synaesthetes in response to the WAT showing breakdown of conventional/unconventional responses

	Synaesthetes			Non-Synaesthetes		
	Conventional	**Unconventional**	**Total**	**Conventional**	**Unconventional**	**Total**
Abstract concepts[a]	5	2	**7**	28	2	**30**
Actions	3	9	**12**	10	0	**10**
Colour [a]	27	38	**65**	11	1	**12**
Synonyms and related emotions [a]	5	0	**5**	43	1	**44**
Exclamations and onomatopoeia	0	1	**1**	5	0	**5**
Nature and natural phenomena	12	13	**25**	10	1	**11**
People, body parts, facial expressions	11	18	**29**	11	2	**13**
Physical objects	5	11	**16**	13	1	**14**
Physical sensations	7	1	**8**	9	3	**12**
Qualities	9	9	**18**	20	2	**22**
Scenarios	0	8	**8**	0	0	**0**
Synaesthetic Association with Letters and Sounds	0	12	**12**	0	0	**0**
Total	**84**	**122**	**206**	**160**	**13**	**173**

([a]significant difference found using a two-tailed test)

significantly more likely to be favoured by one of the groups, we conducted Mann-Whitney *U* Tests. The results are shown in Table 8.

In order to explore the data in more detail, we also ran correlation analyses of the responses produced by the two groups to investigate whether particular types of responses correlated with each other, and whether these relationships held true across the two groups. We are aware that applying such statistical measures to small data sets such as ours is problematic, and that the results should be taken as indicative only, but we considered them a useful way of conceptualising the results and exploring patterns which would not otherwise be

Table 8 Word association response types that were more likely to be favoured by synaesthetes and non-synaesthetes

Response types that were significantly more likely to be provided by synaesthetes, or that were only produced by synaesthetes	Response types that were more frequent in the synaesthetes' data but where the difference was not statistically significant	Response types that were more frequent in the non-synaesthetes' data, but where the difference was not statistically significant	Response types that were significantly more likely to be provided by non-synaesthetes
Colour (two-tailed $U = 82.5$, $n1 = n2 = 20$, $P < 0.05$)	Nature and natural phenomena two-tailed ns one-tailed ns	Qualities two-tailed ns one-tailed ns	Synonyms and related emotions (two-tailed $U = 87$, $n1 = n2 = 20$, $P < 0.05$)
Scenarios (only produced by synaesthetes) two-tailed ns one-tailed ns	People, body parts and facial expressions two-tailed ns one-tailed ns	Physical sensations two-tailed ns one-tailed ns	Abstract concepts (two-tailed $U = 110.5$, $n1 = n2 = 20$, $P < 0.05$)
Synaesthetic associations with letters and sounds (only produced by synaesthetes) two-tailed ns one-tailed ns	Actions two-tailed ns one-tailed ns Physical objects two-tailed ns one-tailed ns	Exclamations and onomato-poeia two-tailed ns one-tailed ns	

apparent. We therefore ran a series of Spearman correlation tests across all association types for each group of participants separately. The results are shown in Tables A13 and A14 in the additional resources.

The responses produced by the synaesthetes demonstrated significant collocations between: abstract concepts and synonyms/related emotions ($\rho = .30$); abstract concepts and nature/natural phenomena ($\rho = .20$); actions and people/body parts/facial expressions ($\rho = .36$); actions and scenarios ($\rho = .58$) and people/body/parts/facial expressions and scenarios ($\rho = .50$). There were significant negative correlations between colour and qualities ($\rho = -.21$), and colour and synaesthetic associations ($\rho = -.33$). The latter finding is particularly interesting as it suggests that when they used colour, the synaesthetes either provided a colour-based synaesthetic association, or they provided a metaphorical colour association, but they rarely combined both strategies. In contrast, there was only one significant correlation found in the non-synaesthetes' data, in which a significant negative correlation was found between synonyms and related emotions and colour ($\rho = -.20$).

These analyses reveal that the responses produced by synaesthetes and non-synaesthetes differ in some notable ways. First, similarly to the writing task, the responses produced by the synaesthetes seem to demonstrate more interrelatedness in the categories they fall into. This is demonstrated by the fact that there are more significant correlations occurring in the synaesthetes' responses. Perhaps the 'interrelatedness' in the categories here is reminiscent of the synaesthetes' neural architecture, characterised as it is by highly levels of connectivity. It is interesting that the category denoting synaesthetic associations with letters and sounds does not correlate positively with any other response types. These associations are perhaps best considered their own separate category, a representation of a synaesthete's own personal and arbitrary associations and perhaps, when triggered, strong enough to override the use of other response categories.

The statistical analyses reported above have enabled us to identify areas where the two groups noticeably differ from each other, and where they overlap. In order to illustrate these response patterns, it is useful at this point to explore the answers provided by some of the synaesthetes in a more qualitative manner. By doing so, we hope to show how the different categories of response related to one another, and how the divergent thinking patterns displayed by synaesthetes manifested when they were performing this task. We consider here (a) response types that were significantly more likely to be provided by synaesthetes, or only produced by them; (b) response types that were more frequent in the synaesthetes' data but where the difference was not statistically significant; (c) response types that were favoured by non-synaesthetes, but where the difference was not statistically significant; and (d) response types that were significantly more likely to be provided by non-synaesthetes. Within each of these categories, we look at the way the two groups differ in their use of the response types in general, and the extent to which these response types were used creatively.

4.3.1 WAT Responses Significantly More Likely to Be Provided by Synaesthetes, or Only Produced by Synaesthetes

Colour

Synaesthetes were significantly more likely to refer to colours as part of their word association task responses, and they were much more likely than the non-synaesthetes to use them in a novel way. In this category, we include responses involving emotion–colour associations that made no reference to the appearance of the word itself. Although a small number of the responses produced by the synaesthetes did involve conventional emotion–colour associations, such as 'anger = red' and 'happiness = yellow', the majority involved unconventional associations, which often involved creative extensions of attested relationships. For example, the response *a burst of yellows and white* to the prompt 'surprise' draws on the conventional relationship between 'surprise' and the colour yellow, but includes an element of activity through the use of the word 'burst'. In some cases, synaesthetes added more colours, or more explicit descriptions of the shade of the colour, as in the response 'brownish green' to 'disgust'. This is in line with previous research that has demonstrated that synaesthetes use significantly more words to describe colours than non-synaesthetes, and that these descriptions draw finer distinctions between different shades (Simner et al., 2005). Cytowic and Eagleman (2009, p. 52) propose that 'Rather than simply possessing a more voluble color vocabulary than nonsynesthetes . . . synesthetes experience qualitatively more varied color experiences and merely attempt to describe them accurately', and our findings suggest that they also incorporate this richness of colour experience into their responses to emotion words.

Sometimes, these extensions were presented through elaborated descriptions.

> *A cutesy version of an irritated face, red puffs of emotion floating out at regular intervals* [anger]
> *A screaming head on a black and red background, turned to look back at the undescribed horror from which it runs* [fear]
> *A table that also functions as a jack-in-the-box, which if cranked will spit up a yellow-and-blue gift box* [surprise]

These examples involve elaborations of conventional associations between red and anger, black and fear, and yellow and surprise. Relationships between emotions and colour involve metaphor to a certain degree (Littlemore et al., forthcoming a), and these examples could be considered to be creative uses of metaphor as they involve the kinds of 'creative realisations of wide-scope mappings' (Pérez-Sobrino et al., 2022) that we discussed in Section 2.

Other unconventional uses of colour by the synaesthetes involved drawing new, unattested relationships between emotions and colours, and are thus reminiscent of metaphors involving 'one-off source domains' (Pérez-Sobrino et al., 2022). For example, this synaesthete's response to 'disgust' draws on the colour pink, and creatively extends this mapping by talking specifically about pink liquid dripping down legs:

> *Neon pink. Pink liquid. Dripping down legs.*

Where non-synaesthetes included colour in their responses, all but one example were deemed to be conventional (e.g. 'red' for anger or 'yellow' for happiness). It is arguably possible to explain the one unconventional colour-related response produced by a non-synaesthete ('white light' for anger), as it perhaps relates to ideas of being 'blinded' by anger or being in a 'blinding' rage.

Scenarios

Scenarios were employed only by the synaesthetes, although there were not many of them in the data (seven in total). They involved elaborate descriptions of the kind of scene that they associated with the emotional prompt. They correlated with the 'actions' and 'people' response types, as we can see in the following example, where a synaesthete employs an action-based scenario involving a person to describe their response to the word 'sadness':

> *A petite girl in a blue uniform sitting on the ground under a covered bus stop, rain falling outside, her umbrella torn up at her side and tears falling onto her grief-wracked body* [sadness]

Here is another example where a synaesthete describes a food service employee's potential reaction to the discovery of some rotting meat in order to describe their reaction to 'disgust':

> *A food service employee holding her hands to her mouth, eyes alternatingly alarmed and shut as tight as possible as she runs for the bathroom, leaving behind the rotting meat she found behind a piece of kitchen equipment* [disgust]

These scenarios both involve an attempt to put oneself in the shoes of a person who is experiencing the emotion, thus conveying a degree of empathy. In some ways, these responses resonate with the heightened degrees of empathy in synaesthetes that we found in the first part of our study. As we saw in Section 1, they may also demonstrate a relationship to creativity, as thinking about how one might react emotionally to a given situation has been shown to play a key role in creative design and problem solving. These responses also involve a degree of metonymic thinking as they employ a single scenario to refer to the whole emotion (Radden & Kövecses, 1999), and the degree of detail involved in these scenarios renders them 'novel' (Carter, 2015). In addition to producing creative metaphor, therefore, synaesthetes also demonstrate creative uses of metonymy.

Synaesthetic Associations

As expected, the synaesthetes were the only participants to report associations that were triggered by the letters or the sounds used in the actual word for the emotion. The majority of their responses in this category made some sort of reference to colour along with another physical characteristic, as we can see in the following examples:

> *This word is pale grey/purple, and feels airy* [happiness]
> *This word is bright yellow, and feels smooth* [surprise]
> *'a' is red and 'e' is green* [anger]

Responses such as these were coded as unconventional, given the personal nature of the associations. Although these kinds of associations were different from the more motivated colour associations discussed above, there may be a link between the fact that the sight of a word can automatically trigger a colour association and the enhanced facility that synaesthetes appear to have with emotion–colour associations more generally.

4.3.2 WAT Response Types That Were More Frequent in the Synaesthetes' Data but Where the Difference Was Not Statistically Significant

Nature and Natural Phenomena

Although the synaesthetes produced more responses related to nature and natural phenomena than the non-synaesthetes (25 responses compared to the non-synaesthetes' 11), this difference was largely driven by one synaesthete who made repeated use of this strategy, so the difference between the two groups was not statistically significant. Several participants (all of whom were synaesthetes) made reference to fire or heat in response to anger, reflecting the embodied metaphor ANGER IS HEAT (Grady, 1997; Lakoff & Johnson, 1980). Many of the associations involved metonymic (cause for effect) references to environmental phenomena, such as the sun (for happiness) or grey clouds (for sadness). These kinds of responses tended to be favoured more by the non-synaesthetes. Non-synaesthetes were also more likely to refer to events that they associated with the emotions concerned (for example, associating 'sadness' with 'death') or to report physical responses to the emotions (for example, associating 'sadness' with 'tears'). Even when synaesthetes provided these literal/metonymic associations, these were more likely to be unconventional than those provided by the non-synaesthetes. For example, one of the synaesthetes made an unconventional association between fear and 'long skinny trees with long skinny branches hanging down', another associated happiness with 'clouds in the morning' and another associated sadness with 'small twigs with too many leaves'.

Thus, even though there was no statistically significant difference between the synaesthetes and the non-synaesthetes in terms of their tendency to refer to nature or natural phenomena in their responses, we note that the synaesthetes made relatively more use of this strategy. We also noted that when doing so, the associations that they provided tended to be more figurative than those of the non-synaesthetes, and even when they provided more literal responses, they were more likely to be unconventional.

People, Body Parts and Facial Expressions

The synaesthetes produced more responses related to people, body parts and facial expressions than the non-synaesthetes (29 versus 13), but again this difference was largely driven by one synaesthete who made repeated use of this strategy, so the difference between the two groups was not statistically significant. As observed in previous categories, responses produced by synaesthetes often involved extended, descriptive, novel scenarios as shown in the following example:

> *A cutesy version of an irritated face, red puffs of emotion floating out at regular intervals* [anger]
> *A person with a frown face looking down their noise at someone* [disgust]

When the non-synaesthetes drew on people-related responses, instead of producing these extended scenarios, they often referred to specific people who evoked the stimulus emotion. For example, three non-synaesthetes gave *family* as a response to 'happiness', and one referred specifically to their son. Non-synaesthetes' responses in this category also involved conventional physical responses to the stimulus emotion, such as *smile/smiley face* for 'happiness' (a response given by four of the non-synaesthetes), but these were shorter and more simple than the extended scenarios that were more likely to be given by the synaesthetes.

Actions

Both groups behaved similarly in terms of the number of times they made reference to actions in their responses. However, there were observable differences in the ways in which each group described these actions. All ten of the actions referred to by the non-synaesthetes represented conventional responses to the stimulus emotion, e.g. *crying* for sadness, *laughing* for happiness or *shaking* for fear. One of the synaesthetes gave a similar response (*recoiling* for fear), but for the other eleven action-related responses produced by the synaesthetes, these actions were elaborated upon in more detail. Synaesthetes were more likely to describe these actions as occurring within extended novel scenarios, as seen in the following examples:

> *A disgusted person wiping first their chest then their pants with something on them* [disgust]
> *A person with a slightly frowning face moving their arms like they're cracking the reins of a horse drawn carriage* [sadness]

This finding suggests that the synaesthetes had higher levels of engagement with the stimuli than the non-synaesthetes, and as we saw above in our discussion of these scenarios, they appeared to be attempting to put themselves in the shoes of an imaginary person who was experiencing the emotion, thus displaying a degree of empathy. Reminiscent of the findings discussed in Section 3, it may be the case that these heightened levels of engagement are driving the synaesthetes' tendencies towards creative output.

Physical Objects

There was very little difference between the two groups in terms of the number of responses falling into the 'physical objects' category: sixteen for the synaesthetes, fourteen for the non-synaesthetes. However, again the synaesthetes were more likely than the non-synaesthetes to offer extended descriptions of the objects, or to refer to objects whose connection to the stimulus emotion was not immediately apparent. For example, while the non-synaesthetes referred to conventional objects that might trigger the emotion (*needles* for 'fear', *dog poo* or *vomit* for 'disgust'), synaesthetes' responses included more unusual objects such as *milky mixture, oil and water resistance, lava lamps* for 'anger', *bacon* for 'fear' or *meringue* for 'happiness'. The motivations for the associations between the object and the emotion were sometimes apparent and involved extensions of conventional associations. For example, synaesthetes' references to *rain boots and umbrellas* for 'sadness' relate to, and extend, conventional relationships between rainy weather and sadness. Again, in comparison with the non-synaesthetes the synaesthetes appeared to be producing more extended, more novel responses, or associations that involved creative extensions of conventional relationships, reflecting higher degrees of personal engagement with the stimuli and higher levels of associative fluency.

4.3.3 WAT Response Types That Were More Frequent in the Non-synaesthetes' Data but Where the Difference Was Not Statistically Significant

Qualities

There was very little difference between the two groups in terms of the number of times they referred to qualities in their responses. However, in keeping with the observations from the previous categories, the associations that the synaesthetes and the non-synaesthetes provided within this category differed in qualitative terms. The associations that the non-synaesthetes provided were more likely to involve literal events that trigger those emotions, as in the following examples:

> *The destruction of our planet's environment and the* ***selfishness*** *and* ***greed*** *of people that has caused it to happen* [anger]
> ***Inefficiency*** [anger]

They were also likely to involve conventional associations, such as *revolting, horrible, vile* or *rancid* for 'disgust'. In contrast, the synaesthetes were more likely to refer to unconventional situations that provoke those emotions, such as, for example, *dripping down legs* or *limbs stretched too far* for 'disgust'.

Physical Sensations

The non-synaesthetes produced more references to physical sensations than the synaesthetes but the difference between the two groups was not statistically significant, largely due to the fact that neither group produced many responses in this category (eight by the synaesthetes, twelve by the non-synaesthetes). However, again, the responses produced by the two groups differed in qualitative terms. The synaesthetes were more likely to provide more detail as to the *location and the quality* of the sensation than the non-synaesthetes; compare the synaesthete's *lifting, warm feeling in my chest* for 'happiness' with the non-synaesthete's *warmth*, for example. Similarly, compare the synaesthete's *jolt of panic through my body* for 'fear' with the non-synaesthete's *cold.* And finally, consider the two descriptions for sadness that were produced by synaesthetes: *sinking feeling in my chest, maybe with the feeling of being on the edge of tears* and *grey-blue heaviness,* which contrast sharply with the non-synaesthete's *pain.* What we appear to have here is a higher level of physical engagement with the emotion on the part of the synaesthetes, which parallels findings reported in Section 3.

Exclamations and Onomatopoeia

There were very few responses in the exclamations and onomatopoeia category, and the majority were produced by non-synaesthetes (one by the synaesthetes, five by the non-synaesthetes), although the numbers are too small for the difference between the groups to be statistically significant. The exclamatory or onomatopoeic responses to stimuli were all entirely conventional, such as *yeurgh, yuck* or *blech* for 'disgust' or *OOOOOOH* for 'surprise'. Only one synaesthete gave an exclamatory response to a stimulus, and even this was more novel than the responses provided by the non-synaesthetes (*With an exclamation point* for the trigger word 'surprise').

4.3.4 Response Types That Were Significantly More Likely to Be Provided by Non-synaesthetes

Synonyms and Related Emotions

Non-synaesthetes were significantly more likely to provide responses that were synonyms for the trigger word itself or emotions that were related to it. For example, for the 'anger' stimulus, non-synaesthetes gave responses such as *cross*, *rage* and *annoyance*. The synaesthetes, on the other hand, did this significantly less frequently, perhaps indicating that they are more likely to give responses that activate other parts of the brain, rather than staying within the same domain. In the few cases where they did provide answers in this category, they tended to be slightly longer and more involved, as we can see in the following example, which was produced by a synaesthete in response to 'disgust':

> *Feeling like flinching away from something* [disgust]

Here the respondent describes a feeling of wanting to undertake a specific physical action in response to the feeling of disgust, which again aligns with previous findings showing that synaesthetes tend to react in a more personal, involved way to the stimuli and to put themselves in the position of someone who is experiencing a given emotion.

Abstract Concepts

Non-synaesthetes produced significantly more responses drawing on abstract concepts than the synaesthetes. However, when they did employ this strategy, non-synaesthetes and synaesthetes alike tended to draw on abstract concepts that triggered the specific emotion acting as a stimulus, or that occurred as a result of it. For example, for the emotion 'anger', non-synaesthetes referred to concepts such as *violence*, loss of control and *the destruction of our planet's environment* as their responses. For synaesthetes, one gave the response *disconnection* for 'sadness'. The majority of these responses were conventional.

4.4 Conclusion

From our analysis of the associations that were favoured by the two groups, and of the qualitative differences between the ways in which the two groups used them, we can see that synaesthetes appear to favour responses that are more novel, more conceptually distant from the prompt, and that they engage with the prompt in a more personal or embodied way than the non-synaesthetes. They tend to provide longer, more detailed answers or extended scenarios that combine all of these features. In contrast, non-synaesthetes tend to favour more conventional associations that relate more closely and more directly to the stimulus. The synaesthetes' response categories were also more likely to be strongly correlated with one another than those of the non-synaesthetes, demonstrating higher levels of interrelatedness. These findings speak to the associative thinking style that is characteristic of synaesthetes, which we discussed in Sections 1 and 3.

These findings suggest that synaesthetes engage with emotions in a somewhat different way to non-synaesthetes. They appear to engage with them on a deeper level and are more likely to relate them to personal physical experiences or interactions with the physical world. Their associations are much more likely to be unconventional. They combine novelty with a degree of appropriacy, which means that they are in a sense 'creative'. In contrast, non-synaesthetes tend not to engage in cross-sensory or cross-domain mappings; they remain within the same conceptual domain, for example by associating one emotion with other related emotions. The ability to form wider sets of unconventional associations based on a broader set of criteria characterises the responses of the synaesthetes and appears to mirror earlier findings discussed in Section 1, which show that synaesthetes display higher levels of associative fluency. However again, like the responses discussed in Section 3, the associations that they form do not appear to be entirely arbitrary; rather, they involve novel elaborations of conventional associations. The tendency to produce these associations demonstrates higher levels of associative fluency in the synaesthete group, which has been shown to be a key factor underpinning metaphor.

5 'I Don't Like Looking at Numbers with No Discernible Pattern': Conclusion

In this book we have explored what synaesthesia can tell us the ability or propensity to produce creative metaphor. We have done this by conducting an in-depth examination of what 'looks like' creative metaphor in the writing of synaesthetes and non-synaesthetes, and identifying features that appear to be associated with this style of thinking. By doing so, we have identified factors that seem to trigger the production of creative metaphor in synaesthetes and, by extension, in the population more generally.

In this respect, the study is the first to do two things. First, it has examined the ways in which synaesthetes and non-synaesthetes experience positive and negative sensory phenomena involving all five senses, and second, it has explored the language that they use when describing these experiences. It has been noted in the literature that synaesthetes have much richer responses to sensory phenomena, but our study is the first to detail the nature of this complexity, to explore how responses vary according to the valence of the phenomena, and to examine the extent to which all of this is reflected in synaesthetes' written descriptions of their experiences. This study is also novel from a methodological perspective as it involves qualitative and quantitative analysis of actual writings produced by synaesthetes.

We have provided linguistic evidence which corroborates some of the findings that have been made in more experimental studies. These include the tendency for synaesthetes to personify stimuli (e.g. Amin et al., 2011) and subsequently empathise with them (Smilek et al., 2007). Our findings also support and build upon previous work on the emotional responses that synaesthetes have to sensory phenomena. Ramachandran and Brang (2008) found that in tactile-emotion synaesthesia, textures elicit emotional responses, whereas in our study we have shown that synaesthetes of all types are more likely than non-synaesthetes to experience emotional responses to a range of phenomena, regardless of sense.

The synaesthetes in our study tended to make value judgements about sensory stimuli, a finding which builds on previous work that has shown that synaesthetes tend to have negative reactions to stimuli that go against their own cross-sensory mappings (Safran & Sanda, 2015). In this study, we have found a tendency for synaesthetes to attach 'moral' judgements to sensory experiences directly, regardless of the cross-sensory activation. For example, stronger flavours can be deemed 'worthwhile', or burning leaves can smell 'wrong' for synaesthetes.

Our study has also revealed three categories of response that have not been revealed in the literature on synaesthesia to date. These are: cognitive effects (where participants described an object or experience which had an effect on the way they thought), physical effects (where participants described having a physical, bodily response to the object or experience under consideration) and hyperbole (where participants described extreme positive or negative reactions to sensory experiences). We found that synaesthetes were significantly more likely to produce these three types of responses than non-synaesthetes. While both groups produced more response types for negative sensory experiences, the trend towards negativity was slightly stronger in the non-synaesthetes than for the synaesthetes. Taken together, all these findings build up a picture of synaesthetes tending towards producing responses that are richer, more descriptive, and that draw on a larger variety of interrelated response types. We have argued that this may reflect a certain intensity to their experiences, and an increased desire to communicate them effectively.

One of the most important findings of the study is that synaesthetes are significantly more likely than non-synaesthetes to use more metaphor in their descriptions of sensory experiences, much of which appears to be highly creative, and that they were particularly likely to use metaphor to describe positive sensory experiences. So, what does this tell us about the relationship between metaphor, emotion and creativity? As we saw in Section 1, it has been suggested that synaesthesia provides a lens through which to examine creativity, specifically metaphorical creativity (Cytowic, 2013; Ramachandran & Brang, 2013). Creativity may best be considered a natural emerging phenomenon from strong and unusual sensory and emotional experiences, and a desire to communicate these experiences. We saw in Section 1 that people have been shown to produce more creative metaphor when describing or evaluating personal and significant emotional experiences, and that this propensity reflects the links that have been identified between emotion, cognition and sensory activation (Damasio, 1994). In this research, we have demonstrated that these connections are made manifest in the writing produced by synaesthetes. Both groups produced creative metaphor when asked to describe their experiences, but the synaesthetes did so significantly more often than the non-synaesthetes. At the same time the characteristics of their responses indicated that they were responding to the task in a much more personal, involved and emotional way than the non-synaesthetes. It appears to be this level of engagement that is driving the creative process in the synaesthetes. In the same way as the emotions experienced by Lubart and Getz's business students drove them to produce creative yet apt metaphor (see Section 1), the emotional reactions experienced by the synaesthetic participants in our study (in particular the positive ones) led them to provide creative, metaphorical descriptions of sensory experiences.

These findings were mirrored in the word association task (see Section 4), which showed that the synaesthetes tended to make associations that were more novel, more conceptually distant from the prompt, and demonstrated more personal or embodied engagement than the non-synaesthetes. Reminiscent of the findings from the extended writing task, the synaesthetes' response categories were also more likely to be strongly correlated with one another than those of the non-synaesthetes, demonstrating higher levels of interrelatedness. Their responses were also longer, demonstrating higher levels of engagement with the prompts. Thus, emotional prompts trigger a wider range of associations in synaesthetes than in non-synaesthetes, demonstrating a certain richness in synaesthetes' responses to emotion, alongside higher levels of associative fluency. This provides further support for the notion that rich, personal emotional experiences trigger associative thinking patterns, which in turn drive creative metaphor production, and that this tendency is particularly marked for synaesthetes.

To sum up, through the analyses described in this book, we have identified a set of traits that appear to trigger the production of what looks like creative metaphor in communication about sensory experiences and emotions. In both tasks, we have seen a strong propensity in synaesthetes towards what looks like 'creativity', often involving motivated extensions of conventional metaphors. This is highly related to reports of strong, often extreme, emotional reactions that often involve physical or cognitive effects, and to a high level of engagement with the prompt, be it sensory or emotional. Synaesthetes are also more likely to demonstrate a degree of personal identification with the object under discussion, even if it is not a human object. They sometimes adopt a 'moral' standpoint, with firm views on what 'ought' and 'ought not' to be. This cluster of features appears to be feeding into their propensity to produce what looks like creative, cross-sensory metaphor.

Synaesthesia provides for a 'richer world of experience than normal' (Meier & Rothen, 2013, p. 692) and the production of creative metaphors by synaesthetes appears to be a natural response to this richness of experience. We began our study by taking up Ramachandran and Brang's (2013, p. 1017) question of whether 'synaesthesia can give us vital clues toward understanding some of the physiological mechanisms underlying some of the most elusive yet cherished aspects of the human mind', namely the ability or propensity to produce creative metaphor. We would suggest that the associative fluency that serves as a necessary starting point for this is most likely to be triggered by strong affective reactions to sensory and emotional stimuli and that one might expect to find an embodied symbiotic relationship in the population as a whole between sensory experiences, emotion, embodiment, hyperbole, empathy, metaphor and creativity.

References

Amin, M., Olu-Lafe, O., Claessen, L. E. et al. (2011). Understanding grapheme personification: A social synaesthesia? *Journal of Neuropsychology, 5*(2), 255–82.

Asher, J. E., Aitken, M. R., Farooqi, N., Kurmani, S., & Baron-Cohen, S. (2006). Diagnosing and phenotyping visual synaesthesia: A preliminary evaluation of the revised test of genuineness (TOG-R). *Cortex, 42*(2), 137–46.

Asher, J. E., & Carmichael, D. A. (2013). The genetics and inheritance of synesthesia. In J. Simner & E. M. Hubbard (Eds.), *The Oxford Handbook of Synesthesia* (pp. 23–45). Oxford: Oxford University Press.

Attardo, S. (2010). *Humorous Texts: A Semantic and Pragmatic Analysis*. Berlin: Walter de Gruyter.

Banissy, M. J., & Ward, J. (2007). Mirror-touch synesthesia is linked with empathy. *Nature Neuroscience, 10*(7), 815–16.

Banissy, M. J., & Ward, J. (2013). Mechanisms of self-other representations and vicarious experiences of touch in mirror-touch synesthesia. *Frontiers in Human Neuroscience, 7*, 112, 1–3.

Barnden, J. (2018). Broadly reflexive relationships, a special type of hyperbole, and implications for metaphor and metonymy. *Metaphor and Symbol, 33*(3), 218–34.

Barnden, J. (2020). Uniting irony, hyperbole and metaphor in an affect-centred pretence-based framework. In A. Athanasiadou & H. L. Colston (Eds.), *The Diversity of Irony* (pp. 15–65). Berlin: De Gruyter Mouton.

Barnden, J. A., Glasbey, S. R., Lee, M. G., & Wallington, A. M. (2003). Domain-transcending mappings in a system for metaphorical reasoning. *Conference Companion of the 10th Conference of the European Chapter of the Association for Computational Linguistics* (EACL 2003), 57–61.

Barsalou, L. W. (1999). Perceptual symbol systems. *Behavioral and Brain Sciences, 22*(4), 577–660.

Bastian, B. (2017). A social dimension to enjoyment of negative emotion in art reception. *Behavioural and Brain Sciences, 40*. www.proquest.com/docview/1988261614?pq-origsite=gscholar&fromopenview=true

Blakemore, S.-J., Bristow, D., Bird, G., Frith, C., & Ward, J. (2005). Somatosensory activations during the observation of touch and a case of vision–touch synaesthesia. *Brain, 128*(7), 1571–83.

Boulenger, V., Hauk, O., & Pulvermüller, F. (2009). Grasping ideas with the motor system: Semantic somatotopy in idiom comprehension. *Cerebral Cortex, 19*(8), 1905–14. https://doi.org/10.1093/cercor/bhn217.

Brang, D., & Ramachandran, V. S. (2011). Survival of the synesthesia gene: Why do people hear colors and taste words? *PLoS Biology*, *9*(11), e1001205.

Bruxner, G. (2015). 'Mastication rage': A review of misophonia – an under-recognised symptom of psychiatric relevance? *Australasian Psychiatry*, *24*(2), 195–7. https://doi.org/10.1177/1039856215613010.

Caballero, R. (2009). Cutting across the senses: Imagery in winespeak and audiovisual promotion. In C. Forceville & E. Urios-Aparisi (Eds.), *Multimodal Metaphor* (pp. 73–94). Berlin: De Gruyter Mouton.

Cacciari, C., Bolognini, N., Senna, I. et al. (2011). Literal, fictive and metaphorical motion sentences preserve the motion component of the verb: A TMS study. *Brain and Language*, *119*(3), 149–57.

Callejas, A., & Lupiáñez, J. (2013). Synesthesia, incongruence, and emotionality. In J. Simner & E. Hubbard (Eds.), *The Oxford Handbook of Synesthesia* (pp. 347–66). Oxford: Oxford University Press.

Cameron, L., & Deignan, A. (2003). Combining large and small corpora to investigate tuning devices around metaphor in spoken discourse. *Metaphor and Symbol*, *18*(3), 149–60.

Cannon, W. (1929). *Bodily Changes in Pain, Hunger, Fear and Rage: An Account of Recent Research Into the Function of Emotional Excitement* (2nd ed.). New York: Appleton-Century-Crofts.

Cardillo, E. R., Watson, C. E., Schmidt, G. L., Kranjec, A., & Chatterjee, A. (2012). From novel to familiar: Tuning the brain for metaphors. *Neuroimage*, *59*(4), 3212–21.

Carmichael, D. A., Down, M. P., Shillcock, R. C., Eagleman, D. M., & Simner, J. (2015). Validating a standardised test battery for synesthesia: Does the synesthesia battery reliably detect synesthesia? *Consciousness and Cognition*, *33*, 375–85. https://doi.org/10.1016/j.concog.2015.02.001.

Carter, R. (1999). Common language: Corpus, creativity and cognition. *Language and Literature*, *8*(3), 195–216.

Carter, R. (2015). *Language and Creativity: The Art of Common Talk*. London: Routledge.

Chandler, J. J., Reinhard, D., & Schwarz, N. (2012). To judge a book by its weight you need to know its content: Knowledge moderates the use of embodied cues. *Journal of Experimental Social Psychology*, *48*(4), 948–52.

Citron, F. M. M., & Goldberg, A. E. (2014). Metaphorical sentences are more emotionally engaging than their literal counterparts. *Journal of Cognitive Neuroscience*, *26*(11), 2585–95. https://doi.org/10.1162/jocn_a_00654.

Citron, F., & Zervos, E. A. (2018). A neuroimaging investigation into figurative language and aesthetic perception. In A. Baicchi, R. Digonnet, & J. Sandford

(Eds.), *Sensory Perceptions in Language, Embodiment and Epistemology* (pp. 77–94). Berlin: Springer.

Clarke, T., & Costall, A. (2008). The emotional connotations of color: A qualitative investigation. *Color Research & Application*, *33*(5), 406–10. https://doi.org/10.1002/col.20435.

Cohen Kadosh, R., & Henik, A. (2007). Can synaesthesia research inform cognitive science? *Trends in Cognitive Sciences*, *11*(4), 177–84. https://doi .org/10.1016/j.tics.2007.01.003.

Colston, H. L., & Gibbs, R. W. (2021). Figurative language communicates directly because it precisely demonstrates what we mean. *Canadian Journal of Experimental Psychology/Revue Canadienne de Psychologie Expérimentale*. Advance online publication. https://doi.org/10.1037/cep0000254.

Cook, G. (2000). *Language Play, Language Learning*. Oxford: Oxford University Press.

Cytowic, R. (1989). Synesthesia and mapping of subjective sensory dimensions. *Neurology*, *39*(6), 849–50.

Cytowic, R. E. (1994). *The Man Who Tasted Shapes*. London: Abacus.

Cytowic, R. E. (2002). *Synesthesia: A Union of the Senses*. Cambridge, MA: MIT Press.

Cytowic, R. E. (2013). Synesthesia in the twentieth century. In J. Simner & E. Hubbard (Eds.), *The Oxford Handbook of Synesthesia* (pp. 399–408). Oxford: Oxford University Press.

Cytowic, R. E., & Eagleman, D. M. (2009). *Wednesday is Indigo Blue: Discovering the Brain of Synesthesia*. Cambridge, MA: MIT Press.

Dailey, A., Martindale, C., & Borkum, J. (1997). Creativity, synesthesia, and physiognomic perception. *Creativity Research Journal*, *10*(1), 1–8.

Damasio, A. R. (1994). *Descartes' Error: Emotion, Rationality and the Human Brain*. New York: Avon.

Day, S. (1996). Synaesthesia and synaesthetic metaphors. *Psyche*, *2*(32), 1–16.

Degani, M., & Onysko, A. (2021). Cultural metaphors of personification in Aotearoa English. In M. Callies & M. Degani (Eds.), *Metaphor in Language and Culture Across World Englishes* (pp. 219–39). London: Bloomsbury.

Deignan, A., Littlemore, J., & Semino, E. (2013). *Figurative Language, Genre and Register*. Cambridge: Cambridge University Press.

Derman, A., & Eilks, I. (2016). Using a word association test for the assessment of high school students' cognitive structures on dissolution. *Chemistry Education Research and Practice*, *17*(4), 902–13.

Desai, R. H., Binder, J. R., Conant, L. L., Mano, Q. R., & Seidenberg, M. S. (2011). The neural career of sensory-motor metaphors. *Journal of Cognitive Neuroscience*, *23*(9), 2376–86. https://doi.org/10.1162/jocn.2010.21596.

Eagleman, D. M., Kagan, A. D., Nelson, S. S., Sagaram, D., & Sarma, A. K. (2007). A standardized test battery for the study of synesthesia. *Journal of Neuroscience Methods*, *159*(1), 139–45.

Ekman, P. (1992). An argument for basic emotions. *Cognition & Emotion*, *6*(3–4), 169–200.

Fainsilber, L., & Ortony, A. (1987). Metaphorical uses of language in the expression of emotions. *Metaphor and Symbol*, *2*(4), 239–50.

Faust, M., & Kenett, Y. N. (2014). Rigidity, chaos and integration: Hemispheric interaction and individual differences in metaphor comprehension. *Frontiers in Human Neuroscience*, *8*, 511, 1–10.

Fetterman, A. K., Robinson, M. D., & Meier, B. P. (2012). Anger as 'seeing red': Evidence for a perceptual association. *Cognition & Emotion*, *26*(8), 1445–58.

Finke, R. A. (1996). Imagery, creativity, and emergent structure. *Consciousness and Cognition*, *5*(3), 381–93.

Foolen, A. (2012). The relevance of emotion for language and linguistics. In A. Foolen, U. Lüdtke, T. Racine, & J. Zlatev (Eds.), *Moving Ourselves, Moving Others: Motion and Emotion in Intersubjectivity, Consciousness and Language* (pp. 349–69). Amsterdam: John Benjamins.

Fuoli, M., Littlemore, J., & Turner, S. (2021). Sunken ships and screaming banshees: Metaphor and evaluation in film reviews. *English Language and Linguistics*, *26*(1), 75–103. https://doi.org/10.1017/S1360674321000046.

Furnham, A. (1986). Response bias, social desirability and dissimulation. *Personality and Individual Differences*, *7*(3), 385–400. https://doi.org/10.1016/0191-8869(86)90014-0.

Gibbs, R. W. (1994). *The Poetics of Mind: Figurative Thought, Language, and Understanding*. Cambridge: Cambridge University Press.

Gibbs, R. W. (2015). Does deliberate metaphor theory have a future? *Journal of Pragmatics*, *90*, 73–6.

Gibbs, R. W. (2017). *Metaphor Wars*. Cambridge: Cambridge University Press.

Gibbs, R. W., & Franks, H. (2002). Embodied metaphor in women's narratives about their experiences with cancer. *Health Communication*, *14*(2), 139–65.

Grady, J. (1997). *Foundations of Meaning: Primary Metaphors and Primary Scenes*. PhD dissertation, University of California, Berkeley.

Grady, J. (2019). A typology of motivation for conceptual metaphor: Correlation vs. resemblance. In R. Gibbs & G. Steen (Eds.), *Metaphor in Cognitive Linguistics* (pp. 79–100). Amsterdam: John Benjamins.

Gray, B. F., & Simner, J. (2015). Synesthesia and release phenomena in sensory and motor grounding: Cases of disinhibited embodiment? *Frontiers in Psychology*, *6*, 54, 1–4.

Hubbard, E. M. (2007). Neurophysiology of synesthesia. *Current Psychiatry Reports*, *9*(3), 193–9.

Jing-Schmidt, Z. (2007). Negativity bias in language: A cognitive-affective model of emotive intensifiers. *Cognitive Linguistics*, *18*(3), 417–43. https://doi.org/10.1515/COG.2007.023.

Jonas, C., & Jarick, M. (2013). Synesthesia, sequences, and space. In J. Simner & E. Hubbard (Eds.), *The Oxford Handbook of Synesthesia* (pp. 123–47). Oxford: Oxford University Press.

Kaya, N., & Epps, H. H. (2004). Relationship between color and emotion: A study of college students. *College Student Journal*, *38*(3), 396–405.

Kenett, Y. N., & Faust, M. (2019). A semantic network cartography of the creative mind. *Trends in Cognitive Sciences*, *23*(4), 271–4. https://doi.org/10.1016/j.tics.2019.01.007.

Lacey, S., Stilla, R., & Sathian, K. (2012). Metaphorically feeling: Comprehending textural metaphors activates somatosensory cortex. *Brain and Language*, *120*(3), 416–21. https://doi.org/10.1016/j.bandl.2011.12.016.

Lakoff, G., & Johnson, M. (1980). *Metaphors We Live By*. Chicago: University of Chicago Press.

Lakoff, G., & Turner, M. (2009). *More than Cool Reason: A Field Guide to Poetic Metaphor*. Chicago: University of Chicago Press.

Latorres, J., Mitterer-Daltoé, M., & Queiroz, M. (2016). Hedonic and word association techniques confirm a successful way of introducing fish into public school meals. *Journal of Sensory Studies*, *31*(3), 206–12.

Lee, K.-W. (1988). Two non-traditional measures of chemistry learning: Word association and idea association. *Research in Science Education*, *18*(1), 169–76.

Lindborg, P., & Friberg, A. K. (2015). Colour association with music is mediated by emotion: Evidence from an experiment using a CIE Lab interface and interviews. *PloS One*, *10*(12), e0144013.

Littlemore, J., Bolognesi, M., Julich, N., Leung, D., & Pérez-Sobrino, P. (forthcoming a). *Metaphor, Metonymy, the Body and the Environment: An Exploration of the Factors that Shape Emotion-Colour Associations and Their Variation across Cultures*. Cambridge: Cambridge University Press.

Littlemore, J., & Low, G. D. (2006). *Figurative Thinking and Foreign Language Learning*. Basingstoke: Palgrave Macmillan.

Littlemore, J., & Turner, S. (2019). Metaphors in communication about pregnancy loss. *Metaphor and the Social World*, *10*(1), 45–75.

Littlemore, J., Turner, S., & Tuck, P. (forthcoming b). *Creative Metaphor, Emotion and Evaluation in Conversations about Work*. London: Routledge.

Lubart, T. I., & Getz, I. (1997). Emotion, metaphor, and the creative process. *Creativity Research Journal*, *10*(4), 285–301. https://doi.org/10.1207/s15326934crj1004_1.

MacCormac, E. R. (1986). Creative metaphors. *Metaphor and Symbol*, *1*(3), 171–84.

Maister, L., Banissy, M. J., & Tsakiris, M. (2013). Mirror-touch synaesthesia changes representations of self-identity. *Neuropsychologia*, *51*(5), 802–8.

Majid, A., Roberts, S. G., Cilissen, L. et al. (2018). Differential coding of perception in the world's languages. *Proceedings of the National Academy of Sciences*, *115*(45), 11369–76.

Marks, L. E. (2013). Weak synesthesia in perception and language. In J. Simner & E. Hubbard (Eds.), *The Oxford Handbook of Synesthesia* (pp. 761–89). Oxford: Oxford University Press.

Martin, J. R., & White, P. R. R. (2005). *The Language of Evaluation: Appraisal in English*. London: Palgrave Macmillan.

Maurer, D., Gibson, L. C., & Spector, F. (2013). Synesthesia in infants and very young children. In J. Simner & E. Hubbard (Eds.), *The Oxford Handbook of Synesthesia* (pp. 46–53). Oxford: Oxford University Press.

Maurer, D., & Mondloch, C. J. (2005). Neonatal synesthesia: A reevaluation. In L. Robertson & N. Sagiv (Eds.), *Synesthesia: Perspectives from Cognitive Neuroscience* (pp. 193–213). Oxford: Oxford University Press.

Meier, B., & Rothen, N. (2013). Synaesthesia and memory. In J. Simner & E. Hubbard (Eds.), *The Oxford Handbook of Synesthesia* (pp. 692–706). Oxford: Oxford University Press.

Mitchell, K. J. (2013). Synesthesia and cortical connectivity. In J. Simner & E. Hubbard (Eds.), *The Oxford Handbook of Synesthesia* (pp. 530–50). Oxford: Oxford University Press.

Mulvenna, C. M. (2013). Synesthesia and creativity. In J. Simner & E. Hubbard (Eds.), *The Oxford Handbook of Synesthesia* (pp. 607–30). Oxford: Oxford University Press.

Musolff, A. (2016). *Political Metaphor Analysis: Discourse and Scenarios*. London: Bloomsbury.

Neufeld, J., Sinke, C., Dillo, W. et al. (2012). The neural correlates of coloured music: A functional MRI investigation of auditory–visual synaesthesia. *Neuropsychologia*, *50*(1), 85–9. https://doi.org/10.1016/j.neuropsychologia.2011.11.001.

Norrick, N. R. (2004). Hyperbole, extreme case formulation. *Journal of Pragmatics*, *36*(9), 1727–39.

Palmer, S. E., Schloss, K. B., Xu, Z., & Prado-León, L. R. (2013). Music–color associations are mediated by emotion. *Proceedings of the National Academy of Sciences*, *110*(22), 8836–41.

Pérez-Sobrino, P., Semino, E., Ibarretxe-Antuñano, I., Koller, V., & Olza, I. (2022). Acting like a hedgehog in times of pandemic: Metaphorical creativity in the #reframecovid collection. *Metaphor and Symbol*, *37*(2), 127–39.

Piaget, J. (2002). *The Language and Thought of the Child* (3rd ed.). London: Routledge.

Poerio, G. L., Blakey, E., Hostler, T. J., & Veltri, T. (2018). More than a feeling: Autonomous sensory meridian response (ASMR) is characterized by reliable changes in affect and physiology. *PloS One*, *13*(6), e0196645. https://doi.org/10.1371/journal.pone.0196645.

Pragglejaz. (2007). MIP: A method for identifying metaphorically used words in discourse. *Metaphor and Symbol*, *22*(1), 1–40.

Radden, G., & Kövecses, Z. (1999). Towards a theory of metonymy. In K. Panther & G. Radden (Eds.), *Metonymy in Language and Thought* (pp. 17–60). Amsterdam: John Benjamins.

Ramachandran, V. S., & Brang, D. (2008). Tactile-emotion synesthesia. *Neurocase*, *14*(5), 390–9.

Ramachandran, V. S., & Brang, D. (2013). From molecules to metaphor: Outlooks on synesthesia research. In J. Simner & E. Hubbard (Eds.), *The Oxford Handbook of Synesthesia* (pp. 999–1021). Oxford: Oxford University Press.

Ramachandran, V. S., & Hubbard, E. M. (2005). The emergence of the human mind: Some clues from synesthesia. In L. Robertson & N. Sagiv (Eds.), *Synesthesia: Perspectives from Cognitive Neuroscience* (pp. 147–90). Oxford: Oxford University Press.

Raskin, V. (1985). *Semantic Mechanisms of Humor*. Dordrecht: D. Reidel.

Rojas-Rivas, E., Espinoza-Ortega, A., Martínez-García, C. G., Moctezuma-Pérez, S., & Thomé-Ortiz, H. (2018). Exploring the perception of Mexican urban consumers toward functional foods using the Free Word Association technique. *Journal of Sensory Studies*, *33*(5), e12439.

Ronga, I. (2016). Taste synaesthesias: Linguistic features and neurophsysiological bases. In E. Gola & F. Ervas (Eds.), *Metaphor and Communication* (pp. 47–60). Amsterdam: John Benjamins.

Rothen, N., Berry, C. J., Seth, A. K., Oligschläger, S., & Ward, J. (2020). A single system account of enhanced recognition memory in synaesthesia. *Memory & Cognition*, *48*(2), 188–99.

Rothen, N., & Meier, B. (2010). Higher prevalence of synaesthesia in art students. *Perception*, *39*(5), 718–20.

Rouw, R. (2013). Synesthesia, hyperconnectivity, and diffusion tensor imaging. In J. Simner & E. Hubbard (Eds.), *The Oxford Handbook of Synesthesia* (pp. 500–18). Oxford: Oxford University Press.

Rouw, R., & Scholte, H. S. (2007). Increased structural connectivity in grapheme-color synesthesia. *Nature Neuroscience*, *10*(6), 792–7.

Rozin, P., & Royzman, E. B. (2001). Negativity bias, negativity dominance, and contagion. *Personality and Social Psychology Review*, *5*(4), 296–320. https://doi.org/10.1207/S15327957PSPR0504_2.

Runco, M. A., & Jaeger, G. J. (2012). The standard definition of creativity. *Creativity Research Journal*, *24*(1), 92–6.

Russ, S. W. (2013). *Affect and Creativity: The Role of Affect and Play in the Creative Process*. London: Routledge.

Safran, A. B., & Sanda, N. (2015). Color synesthesia: Insight into perception, emotion, and consciousness. *Current Opinion in Neurology*, *28*(1), 36–44.

Sagiv, N., Sobczak-Edmans, M., & Williams, A. L. (2017). *Personification, Synaesthesia and Social Cognition*. Oxford: Oxford University Press.

Sakamoto, M., & Utsumi, A. (2014). Adjective metaphors evoke negative meanings. *PloS One*, *9*(2), e89008. https://doi.org/10.1371/journal.pone.0089008.

Schneider, I. K., Rutjens, B. T., Jostmann, N. B., & Lakens, D. (2011). Weighty matters: Importance literally feels heavy. *Social Psychological and Personality Science*, *2*(5), 474–8.

Schubert, E. (1996). Enjoyment of negative emotions in music: An associative network explanation. *Psychology of Music*, *24*(1), 18–28.

Seitz, J. A. (2005). The neural, evolutionary, developmental, and bodily basis of metaphor. *New Ideas in Psychology*, *23*(2), 74–95.

Semino, E. (2008). *Metaphor in Discourse*. Cambridge: Cambridge University Press.

Semino, E. (2011). Metaphor, creativity, and the experience of pain across genres. In J. Swann, R. Pope, & R. Carter (Eds.), *Creativity in Language and Literature: The State of the Art* (pp. 83–102). Basingstoke: Palgrave Macmillan.

Serres, M. (2008). *The Five Senses: A Philosophy of Mingled Bodies*. London: Continuum.

Shaw, G. (2008). The multisensory image and emotion in poetry. *Psychology of Aesthetics, Creativity, and the Arts*, *2*(3), 175–8.

Shelley, P. B. (1898). *The Sensitive Plant*. London: Aldine House.

Shen, Y. (1997). Cognitive constraints on poetic figures. *Cognitive Linguistics*, *8*, 33–71.

Shen, Y., & Cohen, M. (1998). How come silence is sweet but sweetness is not silent: A cognitive account of directionality in poetic synaesthesia. *Language and Literature*, *7*(2), 123–40. https://doi.org/10.1177/096394709800700202.

Simner, J. (2007). Beyond perception: Synaesthesia as a psycholinguistic phenomenon. *Trends in Cognitive Sciences*, *11*(1), 23–9. https://doi.org/10.1016/j.tics.2006.10.010.

Simner, J. (2013). The 'rules' of synesthesia. In J. Simner & E. Hubbard (Eds.), *The Oxford Handbook of Synesthesia* (pp. 149–64). Oxford: Oxford University Press.

Simner, J., & Haywood, S. L. (2009). Tasty non-words and neighbours: The cognitive roots of lexical-gustatory synaesthesia. *Cognition*, *110*(2), 171–81.

Simner, J., & Holenstein, E. (2007). Ordinal linguistic personification as a variant of synesthesia. *Journal of Cognitive Neuroscience*, *19*(4), 694–703.

Simner, J., & Hubbard, E. M. (2006). Variants of synesthesia interact in cognitive tasks: Evidence for implicit associations and late connectivity in cross-talk theories. *Neuroscience*, *143*(3), 805–14.

Simner, J., & Hubbard, E. M. (2013a). Overview of terminology and findings. In J. Simner & E. Hubbard (Eds.), *The Oxford Handbook of Synesthesia* (pp. xix–xxvi). Oxford: Oxford University Press.

Simner, J., & Hubbard, E. M. (2013b). Synesthesia in school-aged children. In J. Simner & E. Hubbard (Eds.), *The Oxford Handbook of Synesthesia* (pp. 64–82). Oxford: Oxford University Press.

Simner, J., Mulvenna, C., Sagiv, N. et al. (2006). Synaesthesia: The prevalence of atypical cross-modal experiences. *Perception*, *35*(8), 1024–33. https://doi.org/10.1068/p5469.

Simner, J., Ward, J., Lanz, M. et al. (2005). Non-random associations of graphemes to colours in synaesthetic and non-synaesthetic populations. *Cognitive Neuropsychology*, *22*(8), 1069–85. https://doi.org/10.1080/02643290500200122.

Smilek, D., Malcolmson, K. A., Carriere, J. S. et al. (2007). When '3' is a jerk and 'E' is a king: Personifying inanimate objects in synesthesia. *Journal of Cognitive Neuroscience*, *19*(6), 981–92.

Soares, E. K., Esmerino, E. A., Ferreira, M. V. S. et al. (2017). What are the cultural effects on consumers' perceptions? A case study covering coalho cheese in the Brazilian northeast and southeast area using word association. *Food Research International*, *102*, 553–8.

Sobczak-Edmans, M., & Sagiv, N. (2013). Synesthetic personification. In J. Simner & E. Hubbard (Eds.), *The Oxford Handbook of Synesthesia* (pp. 222–38). Oxford: Oxford University Press.

Spector, F., & Maurer, D. (2008). The colour of Os: Naturally biased associations between shape and colour. *Perception*, *37*(6), 841–7.

Speed, L. J., O'Meara, C., Roque, L. S., & Majid, A. (2019). *Perception Metaphors*. Amsterdam: John Benjamins.

Steen, G. (2008). The paradox of metaphor: Why we need a three-dimensional model of metaphor. *Metaphor and Symbol*, *23*(4), 213–41.

Strik Lievers, F. (2015). Synaesthesia: A corpus-based study of cross-modal directionality. *Functions of Language*, *22*(1), 69–95.

Szabó, G., Fazekas, I., Patkós, C. et al. (2018). Investigation of public attitude towards renewable energy sources using word association method in Hungarian settlements. *Journal of Applied Technical and Educational Sciences*, *8*(1), 6–24.

Torrance, P. E. (1966). *Torrance Tests of Creative Thinking*. Bensenville: Scholastic Testing Services.

Turner, S., Littlemore, J., Burgess, M. et al. (2020). The production of time-related metaphors by people who have experienced pregnancy loss. In J. Barden & A. Gargett (Eds.), *Producing Figurative Expression: Theoretical, Experimental and Practical Perspectives* (pp. 389–418). Amsterdam: John Benjamins.

Ullmann, S. (1967). *The Principles of Semantics*. Oxford: Blackwell.

Van Campen, C. (2010). *The Hidden Sense: Synesthesia in Art and Science*. Cambridge, MA: MIT Press.

Van Campen, C. (2013). Synesthesia in the visual arts. In J. Simner & E. Hubbard (Eds.), *The Oxford Handbook of Synesthesia* (pp. 631–46). Oxford: Oxford University Press.

van Leeuwen, T. M. (2013). Individual differences in synesthesia. In J. Simner & E. Hubbard (Eds.), *The Oxford Handbook of Synesthesia* (pp. 241–64). Oxford: Oxford University Press.

Ward, J. (2004). Emotionally mediated synaesthesia. *Cognitive Neuropsychology*, *21*(7), 761–72.

Ward, J., Huckstep, B., & Tsakanikos, E. (2006). Sound-colour synaesthesia: To what extent does it use cross-modal mechanisms common to us all? *Cortex*, *42*(2), 264–80.

Ward, J., Schnakenberg, P., & Banissy, M. J. (2018). The relationship between mirror-touch synaesthesia and empathy: New evidence and a new screening tool. *Cognitive Neuropsychology*, *35*(5–6), 314–32.

Warren, R. (1998). *The Collected Poems of Robert Penn Warren*. Louisiana: Louisiana State University Press.

Williams, J. M. (1976). Synesthetic adjectives: A possible law of semantic change. *Language*, *52*(2), 461–78.

Williams-Whitney, D., Mio, J. S., & Whitney, P. (1992). Metaphor production in creative writing. *Journal of Psycholinguistic Research*, *21*(6), 497–509. https://doi.org/10.1007/BF01067527.

Winner, E. (2018). *How Art Works: A Psychological Exploration*. Oxford: Oxford University Press.

Winter, B. (2014). Horror movies and the cognitive ecology of primary metaphors. *Metaphor and Symbol*, *29*(3), 151–70.

Winter, B. (2016). Taste and smell words form an affectively loaded and emotionally flexible part of the English lexicon. *Language, Cognition and Neuroscience*, *31*(8), 975–88.

Winter, B. (2019). *Sensory Linguistics*. Amsterdam: John Benjamins.

Wise, H. (2003). *The Vocabulary of Modern French: Origins, Structure and Function*. London: Routledge.

Acknowledgements

First and foremost we would like to express our sincere gratitude to all the participants in our study, without whom this book would not have been possible. We are also grateful to Oscar Malt and Ellen Wilding for the research assistance they provided. We would like to thank the series editors, Sarah Duffy and Nick Riches, for their constant encouragement throughout the project. Finally, a big thank you to Isabel Collins and Naveen Prasath at Cambridge University Press for all their support.

Cambridge Elements

Cognitive Linguistics

Sarah Duffy

Northumbria University

Sarah Duffy is Senior Lecturer in English Language and Linguistics at Northumbria University. She has published primarily on metaphor interpretation and understanding, and her forthcoming monograph for Cambridge University Press (co-authored with Michele Feist) explores *Time, Metaphor, and Language* from a cognitive science perspective. Sarah is Review Editor of the journal, *Language and Cognition*, and Vice President of the UK Cognitive Linguistics Association.

Nick Riches

Newcastle University

Nick Riches is a Senior Lecturer in Speech and Language Pathology at Newcastle University. His work has investigated language and cognitive processes in children and adolescents with autism and developmental language disorders, and he is particularly interested in usage-based accounts of these populations.

Editorial Board

About the Series

Cambridge Elements in Cognitive Linguistics aims to extend the theoretical and methodological boundaries of cognitive linguistics. It will advance and develop established areas of research in the discipline, as well as address areas where it has not traditionally been explored and areas where it has yet to become well-established.

Cambridge Elements

Cognitive Linguistics

A full series listing is available at: www.cambridge.org/ECOG

Printed in the United States
by Baker & Taylor Publisher Services